	DATE DUE		

Alien Abductions

New and future titles in the series include:

The Mystery Library

Alien Abductions

Patricia D. Netzley

Lucent Books, Inc.
P.O. Box 289011, San Diego, California

For Matthew, Sarah, and Jacob

Library of Congress Cataloging-in-Publication Data

Netzley, Patricia D.
  Alien abductions / by Patricia D. Netzley.
    p. cm. — (The mystery library)
  Includes bibliographical references and index.
  Summary: Discusses alien abductions including the Hill abduction
case, evaluating abduction stories, the search for physical proof,
abductions and the human mind, and why aliens visit Earth.
  ISBN 1-56006-767-5 (alk. paper)
  1. Alien abduction—Juvenile literature. [1. Alien abduction.
2. Human-alien encounters. 3. Extraterrestrial beings. 4.
Unidentified flying objects.] I. Title. II. Mystery library
(Lucent Books)
  BF2050 .N48 2001
  001.942—dc21

                                               00-009165

Contents

Foreword

In Shakespeare's immortal play, *Hamlet*, the young Danish aristocrat Horatio has clearly been astonished and disconcerted by his encounter with a ghost-like apparition on the castle battlements. "There are more things in heaven and earth," his friend Hamlet assures him, "than are dreamt of in your philosophy."

Many people today would readily agree with Hamlet that the world and the vast universe surrounding it are teeming with wonders and oddities that remain largely outside the realm of present human knowledge or understanding. How did the universe begin? What caused the dinosaurs to become extinct? Was the lost continent of Atlantis a real place or merely legendary? Does a monstrous creature lurk beneath the surface of Scotland's Loch Ness? These are only a few of the intriguing questions that remain unanswered, despite the many great strides made by science in recent centuries.

Lucent Books' Mystery Library series is dedicated to exploring these and other perplexing, sometimes bizarre, and often disturbing or frightening wonders. Each volume in the series presents the best-known tales, incidents, and evidence surrounding the topic in question. Also included are the opinions and theories of scientists and other experts who have attempted to unravel and solve the ongoing mystery. And supplementing this information is a fulsome list of sources for further reading, providing the reader with the means to pursue the topic further.

The Mystery Library will satisfy every young reader's fascination for the unexplained. As one of history's greatest scientists, physicist Albert Einstein, put it:

> The most beautiful thing we can experience is the mysterious. It is the source of all true art and science. He to whom this emotion is a stranger, who can no longer wonder and stand rapt in awe, is as good as dead: his eyes are closed.

Are Alien Abductions Real Events?

According to a poll conducted in the early 1990s by the Roper Organization, over 3 million people suspect that they have had an encounter with alien beings from another planet. Of these, most claim to have seen an unidentified flying object (UFO) that they believe was an alien spaceship. A few hundred claim that they have not only seen a spaceship but also have clear memories of being abducted, studied, and then released by the aliens who piloted the craft. Several thousand more believe they might have been abducted but have no clear memories of the event.

The stories of abductees who claim memories of their experience are remarkably similar; aliens are generally described in the same way by all. Therefore, although not many people believed the first abductees as the number of abduction stories increased, a few scientists decided to investigate the abduction phenomenon more carefully. Today the number of ufologists (experts in all types of UFO-related events) and abduction researchers examining this phenomenon is high. As Kevin P. Randle, Russ Estes, and William P. Cone report in their book *The Abduction Enigma:*

> There are now, literally, hundreds of people engaged in abduction research, trying to learn what is happening. They are building a huge base of data that, when examined properly and scientifically, could provide the clues to explain what is

This painting by Michael Buhler, titled Fire in the Sky, *depicts aliens transporting a man into a UFO. Transportations are a common detail in the stories of many abductees.*

9

Here, aliens are depicted entering a home to abduct a woman. Due to the large number of stories of abductees, several people have become interested in investigating alien abductions.

happening. . . . The amount of data that has been recovered is staggering. There are dozens of books, magazine articles, television shows and documentaries, and even movies about alien abduction. These have been written or produced by those of professional qualifications, by those who have conducted the research and those who have had the experiences. All have provided important clues about alien abduction.[1]

Out of these abduction researchers, four are pioneers in the field: ufologists Budd Hopkins and David Jacobs, who have evaluated several hundred abduction cases; Harvard psychiatrist John Mack, who has interviewed over a hundred abductees; and ufologist Raymond Fowler, whose popular books on abduction were among the first to catch the public's attention. Fowler's interviews with abductees have led him to conclude that alien abductions exist in a physical reality and are not an illusion.

Reports exist from credible, sane persons who claim to have been abducted by creatures described by nonabductee witnesses. Many elements within their abduction accounts have a commonality. . . . In some cases similar physical marks are left on the abductees' bodies. All of these elements provide strong circumstantial evidence that abductions are grounded in reality.[2]

Other experts in alien abduction offer alternative explanations for the phenomenon. Perhaps abductions are part of some mystical or psychological experience that scientists do not yet understand, or perhaps abductees have merely dreamed or imagined their abductions. Well-known skeptic Philip Klass maintains:

> After having spent more than 22 years investigating famous, seemingly mysterious UFO reports—including some of the earliest claims of UFO abduction—I can assure you that there is absolutely no scientifically credible physical evidence to indicate that the earth is being visited by extraterrestrials—let alone that they are abducting people.[3]

But if Klass is wrong and aliens are indeed visiting Earth, what might their reasons be? Many theories have been proposed regarding the aliens' intent. However, as ufologist Michael Mannion points out, there is no way to know for certain the motives of an extraterrestrial visitor.

> The story of the interaction between European explorers and the indigenous peoples of the New World can be instructive here. When the Europeans arrived in their sailing ships, many of the indigenous peoples interpreted the appearance of these newcomers in terms of their religious mythology. At first, they invested the Europeans with "superior" or even "godly" attributes on the basis of their sudden mysterious appearance and on their advanced technology. . . . [T]he arrival of these

unknown lifeforms seemed to have a "meaning" in relation to their belief systems. However, the Europeans came to the Americas for reasons of their own, which had nothing at all to do with the indigenous peoples. The religious-mystical interpretation of the arrival of Europeans on their shores contributed to the downfall of the existing cultures. The visitors were not gods or advanced beings; they were simply other flawed lifeforms in their own state of evolution.[4]

This comparison leads Mannion to suggest that humans not jump to conclusions regarding the aliens' motives.

Human beings ought to refrain from ascribing a meaning to their arrival. In addition, it is not wise to invest the unknown nonhuman intelligences with any superior or godly attributes, especially on the basis of the advanced technology they appear to possess. . . . Advanced entities may be studying us, but they are not necessarily inherently superior. Most likely they are merely other natural expressions of the Life Energy in the Universe, exploring creation. Whatever they may be, no good can come from mistaking these entities for something they are not. This can only block true understanding of who they may be.[5]

But who might these aliens be? Are they real, or are they some product of the human mind? If real, are they necessarily extraterrestrial? Perhaps they are humans visiting from the future, or beings who come from an alternate reality on Earth. And why do some people experience alien abductions while others do not? Are abductees special in some way? Examining current research into alien abductions does show some commonalities among abductees and the stories they tell. But while these commonalities have led to many theories regarding alien abductions, the phenomenon remains a mystery for those who want definitive proof of its origin.

Chapter 1

Suspecting Abduction: The Hill Case

On the night of September 19, 1961, Betty and Barney Hill were driving along a deserted road from Canada to their home in Portsmouth, New Hampshire. The sky was full of stars. Suddenly, they noticed a strange light moving rapidly across the heavens. They stopped their car several times to study the object through binoculars. It kept changing direction and appeared to have lights on only one side. As it spun around, these lights seemed to wink on and off, and Betty became excited. She decided she had to be seeing a UFO. But Barney disagreed, insisting that the lights had to be coming from an airplane. Then the object came closer, and Barney's doubts were erased. In a letter to Major Donald Keyhoe, founder of the National Investigations Committee on Aerial Phenomena, Betty tells why:

Betty and Barney Hill say they saw a UFO while driving home one night. The couple claims they drove away, but did not escape the spaceship, and were abducted.

As it approached our car, we stopped again. As it hovered in the air in front of us, it appeared to be pancake in shape, ringed with windows in the front through which we could see bright blue-white lights. Suddenly, two red lights appeared on each side. By this time my husband was standing in the road, watching closely [through binoculars]. He saw wings protrude on each side and the red lights were on the wing tips.

As it glided closer he was able to see inside this object, but not too closely. He did see several figures scurrying about as though they were making some hurried type of preparation. One figure was observing us from the windows. From the distance this was seen, the figures appeared to be about the size of a pencil [held at arm's length], and seemed to be dressed in some type of shiny black uniform.[6]

Upon seeing the figures, Barney became terrified. In fact, according to Betty, he was "in a hysterical condition, laughing and repeating that they were going to capture us."[7] The two drove away from the object as fast as they could, and they believed they escaped it. Later, however, they realized that two hours of their time was unaccounted for—"missing"—and they could not remember driving a thirty-five-mile stretch of road. What had happened to those missing two hours? Why did they suddenly find themselves driving thirty-five miles further down the highway?

Missing Time

Missing time is often the first clue that an abduction experience has taken place. Many abductees have lost anywhere from an hour or two to a day or more, and at the end of the episode they frequently find themselves in an unexpected place with no memory of how they got there. To abductees, this is proof that something unusual has happened to them, even if they can't recall the experience itself.

Of course, many people lose track of time, and when this happens while driving it is not unusual for them to return to awareness several miles down the road. As skeptic Philip Klass points out in regard to the Hills:

> If a UFO was indeed following them as they drove along Highway 3, as both . . . suspected, it would be logical to divert to a less conspicuous road. (Later, Betty would recall that they had turned off onto Highway 175, and later onto an obscure side road. Perhaps they had even pulled off the road in the hope they could shake the UFO.)
>
> Considering these diversions and time spent later trying to find their way back to the main highway, it is not surprising that they arrived back in Portsmouth roughly two hours later than originally expected.[8]

But despite alternative explanations for missing time, abduction researchers suspect alien contact whenever a person comes to them reporting such an incident. Therefore these researchers have interpreted the results of a 1992 Gallup poll in which 13 percent of the six thousand respondents reported experiencing at least an hour of missing time as proof that the abduction phenomenon is widespread. When missing time is accompanied by dreams of aliens, abduction researchers are usually certain they have found a bona fide case of alien abduction.

Betty and Barney Hill had such dreams. When they returned home after their UFO encounter, they did not remember anything other than seeing an alien spacecraft in the sky, yet Betty dreamed repeatedly of an abduction experience. According to John G. Fuller, who interviewed the couple for his book *The Interrupted Journey:*

Donald E. Keyhoe, a believer in UFOs. Betty Hill contacted Keyhoe when first she began to believe she had experienced abduction.

Some ten days after the sighting, Betty began having a series of vivid dreams. They continued for five successive nights. Never in her memory had she recalled dreams of such detail and intensity. They dominated her waking life during that week and continued to plague her afterward. But they stopped abruptly after five days, and never returned again. In a sense, they assumed the proportion of nightmares. . . .

Her dreams were unusual in subject matter and detail. They revealed that she encountered a strange roadblock on a lonely New Hampshire road as a group of men approached the car. The men were dressed alike. As soon as they reached the car, she slipped into unconsciousness. She awoke to find herself and Barney being taken aboard a wholly strange craft, where she was given a complete physical examination by intelligent, humanoid beings. Barney was taken off down a corridor, curving to the contour of the ship, for apparently the same reason. They were assured, in the dream, that no harm would come to them and that they would be released without any conscious memory of the strange happening.[9]

It was these dreams that prompted Betty to write to Major Donald Keyhoe, a believer in UFOs and author of a book she had read on the subject, *The Flying Saucer Conspiracy.* Her letter eventually led ufologists to interview the Hills. Meanwhile, Barney began showing the symptoms of emotional distress. After he suffered panic attacks and developed an ulcer he decided to seek psychiatric help to discover the cause of his condition. It was during his sessions with a psychiatrist that first Barney and then Betty became convinced that they had spent their missing two hours aboard an alien spacecraft.

Post-Abduction Syndrome

Betty's dreams and Barney's distress are consistent with Post-Abduction Syndrome (PAS), a specific collection of psychological symptoms that appear in people who claim to have been abducted by aliens. PAS can be mild or severe, depending on the individual abductee. Many PAS sufferers experience anxiety and depression, becoming extremely upset over small problems. They might also have irrational fears. Most PAS sufferers are afraid to be alone and are particularly frightened by deserted roads or fields. Abduction researcher David Jacobs explains:

> [Abductees] may have traveled the same route for years without giving it a thought, but one day they become inordinately afraid of it. They stop traveling on that stretch of road, and go miles out of their way to avoid it. Child abductees who have played in a nearby park every day suddenly are afraid to go there and never want to play there again. They may have suffered strange missing-time episodes at these places, and they will agonize over what happened to them for many years.[10]

PAS sufferers usually have trouble sleeping. They are afraid to go to bed, and many leave lights or radios on for comfort. As with Betty Hill, if they do manage to sleep, they wake frequently and often have vivid nightmares about strange alien beings. These nightmares sometimes intrude on daily activities. For example, abductee Debbie Jordan found herself reliving her dreams during the day:

> My nightmares had begun to seep into my waking state and I had begun to have what I called flashbacks. I could be involved in the most mundane task with my mind blank and suddenly start to see whole scenes whiz before my eyes as if I were watching them on a movie screen. And I was the unwilling star. Sometimes I would only see eyes. These huge, liquid black eyes, boring a hole through me. At other times I would see whole faces, gray faces with slits for mouths.[11]

Besides PAS, abductees have other things in common. When Betty and Barney Hill regained awareness after their experience, they found themselves miles away from where they should have been. David Jacobs says that many people "come to consciousness . . . miles away from where they should have been—not just down the road but on a completely different highway."[12]

Abductees taken from home can also regain awareness in a different place than the one where their experience began. For example, abductee Patti Layne fell asleep in her room and woke up on her bathroom floor. Debbie Jordan found herself outside. Often an abductee gets out of bed in the morning to discover unexplained grass, leaves, or twigs on his or her clothes or feet. Jacobs reports:

> Many abductees have returned to find oddities about their clothes and bodies. It is not unusual for people to notice that their pajamas or nightgowns are on inside out when they felt certain that they had put them on the correct way the night before. . . . Some abductees have reported that their clothes were draped around a chair when they woke up in the morning.[13]

Other abductees discover strange scars on their bodies. Ufologist Raymond Fowler describes his shock at finding such a mark on himself while taking a shower:

> I stared at the side of my lower leg in astonishment. A disquieting aura of disbelief and denial crept over my transfixed wet body. There, just as plain as could be, was a freshly cut scoop mark. I shut off the shower and felt the perfectly round indentation. There was no pain and no signs of bleeding. It looked like a miniature cookie cutter had removed a perfectly round piece of flesh.[14]

Real Fears

Faced with such evidence, abductees begin to suspect that their dreams about aliens reflect something that actually happened. They want to solve the mystery of their missing time. This was true for Betty and Barney Hill. Three years after sighting the UFO, they decided to undergo hypnosis, a therapist-induced mental state that can help people remember forgotten events. A person under hypnosis answers a series of questions designed to elicit important information.

What the Hills discovered through this process astonished them. They learned that Betty's dreams were memories; aliens had indeed taken them aboard their spaceship, put them in separate rooms, and physically examined them before letting them go. Excited, they decided to share their story with others. In 1965, an article about their abduction appeared

Betty and Barney Hill with the book written about their experience entitled, The Interrupted Journey: Two Lost Hours "Aboard a Flying Saucer."

in a Boston newspaper. The following year, author John Fuller published his book about their case, *The Interrupted Journey: Two Lost Hours "Aboard a Flying Saucer."* When popular *Look* magazine discussed *The Interrupted Journey* in its October 6, 1966, issue, the Hills became famous.

Fuller's book reproduced partial transcripts of the statements the Hills made while under hypnosis. Each one's memories of what happened during the "missing time" were basically the same, although Betty offered far more details. As with her dreams, her abduction experience began when she and Barney saw a group of strange-looking men standing in the middle of the road. Barney stopped the car and its engine immediately died, whereupon the aliens removed the couple from the car. In *The Interrupted Journey*, a hypnotized Betty says:

> I'm thinking I'm asleep . . . I'm asleep, and I've got to wake up. . . . But even though I'm asleep, I'm walking! And there's . . . a couple of men behind me, and then there's Barney. There's a man on each side of him. And my eyes are open . . . but Barney's still asleep. He's walking, and he's asleep. . . . And I turn around, and I say, "Barney! Wake up! *Barney!* Why don't you wake up?" And he doesn't pay any attention. He keeps walking. . . . And then the man walking beside me here says, "Oh, is his name Barney?" . . . And I wouldn't answer him, so he says . . . "Don't be afraid. You don't have any reason to be afraid. We're not going to harm you, but we just want to do some tests. When the tests are over with, we'll take you and Barney back and put you in your car. You'll be on your way back home in no time."[15]

Betty's Physical Examination

Betty then recalled walking up a ramp into a spaceship, where the aliens put Barney in one room and her in another. Betty's next memories were of a physical examination:

> And the examiner opens my eyes, and looks in them with a light and he opens my mouth, and he looks in my throat and my teeth and he looks in my ears, and he turned my head, and he looked in this ear. . . . And then the doctor, the examiner says he wants to do some tests, he wants to check my nervous system. And I am thinking, I don't know how our nervous systems are, but I hope we never have nerve enough to go around kidnapping people right off the highways, as he has done![16]

Betty remembered that the aliens used a strange device to touch her on various parts of her head. Although this part of the examination wasn't painful, other parts were. Betty says:

> So then . . . the examiner has a long needle in his hand . . . and it's bigger than any needle that I've ever seen. And I ask him what he's going to do with it . . . and he said he just wants to put it in my navel, it's just a simple test. And I tell him no, it will hurt, don't do it, don't do it. And I'm crying, and I'm telling him, "It's hurting, it's hurting, take it out, take it out!" And the leader comes over and he puts his hand, rubs his hand in front of my eyes, and he says it will be all right. I won't feel it. And all the pain goes away. The pain goes away, but I'm still sore from where they put that needle. I don't know why they put that needle into my navel. Because I told them they shouldn't do it.[17]

According to Betty, when the aliens finished her physical examination, they showed her a star map. They asked her if she knew where Earth was on the map. She had no

*Betty Hill claims that
during her abduction
her alien abductors
showed her a star map.*

Betty Hill claims that during her abduction her alien abductors showed her a star map.

idea. They asked her more questions and sometimes seemed confused about her answers. For example, they wanted to know what human beings ate but did not understand the word "vegetables." They also puzzled over differences between her and Barney. Betty remembers:

> The examiner said that they could not figure it out—Barney's teeth came out, and mine didn't. I was really laughing, and said Barney had dentures, and I didn't, and that is why his teeth came out. So then they asked me, "What are dentures?" And I said people as they got older lost their teeth. They had to go to a dentist and have their teeth extracted, and they put in dentures. . . . And the leader said, "Well, does this happen to many people?" He . . . acted as if he didn't believe me.[18]

Barney's memories under hypnosis were not as complete as Betty's. Some parts of his abduction experience were missing. Still, he recalled being examined. "I was very afraid to open my eyes. I had been told not to open my eyes, and it would be over with quickly. And I could feel them examining me with their hands . . ."[19] At the end of the abduction, Barney remembered:

> And I think I felt very good because I knew it was over. And again, I was led to the door . . . and [I] went back toward the ramp. And I went down and opened my eyes and kept walking. And I saw my car, and the lights were out. And it was sitting down the road and very dark. And I couldn't understand. I had not turned off the lights. . . . And Betty was coming down the road, and she came around and opened the door.[20]

A Basis for Disbelief

When Dr. Benjamin Simon, the Boston psychiatrist who hypnotized the Hills, heard their full story, he dismissed it as untrue. Dr. Simon could not accept that aliens might exist. Therefore he decided that the Hills' experience had to be some kind of dream-fantasy. Dr. Simon based his conclusion in part on the fact that Betty recalled parts of the experience that Barney did not. To Dr. Simon this meant that they could not both have gone through the same event. As skeptic Philip Klass explains:

> Under regressive hypnosis, which was used as a memory aid, Betty recalled many details of the alleged abduction while Barney could recall very few. This, Dr. Simon emphasized, showed that the alleged abduction was *not* a shared experience. The psychiatrist was at first puzzled over how Barney had acquired even a few details of the incident. But he learned that Betty enjoyed recounting her abduction dreams to friends, neighbors, and UFO investigators and that Barney often was present on those occasions, sometimes reading the newspaper or watching television.[21]

In one of several interviews, the Hills explain the appearance of the UFO as they remember it.

Dr. Simon did believe that the Hills had sighted a UFO in the sky, but he suspected that the source of their abduction story was Betty's dreams. He felt that many things Betty said didn't make sense, as is true with dreams. Klass explains:

[Dr. Simon] found that the tale [Betty] told under regressive hypnosis was essentially identical to her nightmare dreams. When I asked Dr. Simon how he could be sure that the original nightmares were not themselves based on an actual experience, he pointed out a few of the many irrational inconsistencies of the abduction story. He stressed that such inconsistencies are characteristic of dreams.

For example . . . the ETs [extraterrestrials] were familiar enough with earthly gadgets to know how to operate the zipper on her dress. But they were completely baffled by the fact that Barney's teeth could be removed, while Betty's were firmly anchored. Betty said she tried to explain to one of the spacemen that when some people get older they need artificial teeth, but he could not comprehend what was meant by age or the passage of time. Yet later, Betty said, when she was about to leave the flying saucer, the same spaceman said to her, "Wait a minute."[22]

Credible Witnesses

But those who knew the Hills felt that these inconsisten-cies were unimportant or could be explained. They point-ed out that Betty and Barney were both respected, church-going members of their community, active in local and national politics. The Hills were highly credible wit-nesses. As a result, many people decided the couple was telling the truth. For example, Budd Hopkins was an artist and sculptor when he first read about them. Their story led him to become a ufologist.

> As I read about the case in detail—[in] Fuller's book, *The Interrupted Journey*—I began to feel that the Hills were recalling precisely what had happened to them, and the fact that it emerged the way it did, under hypnosis, in two separate accounts, gave it unusual validity. If the UFOs were some kind of spacecraft piloted—if that's the word—by extraterrestrials, perhaps they might be exploring very cautiously, giving us a good long look, picking up "samples" under very safe condi-tions, really studying us at long range before landing and establish-ing contact.[23]

After reading the story of Betty and Barney Hill, Budd Hopkins decided to become a ufologist. He felt the Hills' story was consistent and believable.

Once the Hills became famous, other people said they too had been abducted by aliens. Their abduction stories were remark-ably similar to the Hills'. The same details appeared in many of the accounts. This led more and more ufologists to suspect the experience was real.

As the number of abductees increased, psychiatrists began in-depth studies of the phenomenon. They developed certain guidelines for evaluating abduction stories. They also formed certain conclusions about what might be happening to abductees. Meanwhile, the Hills continued to maintain that their experience was real. John Mack reports:

> Despite Dr. Simon's belief that the Hills had experienced some sort of shared dream or fantasy . . . they persisted in their conviction that these events really happened, and that they had not communicated the corroborating details to each other during the investigation of their symptoms. Barney, who died in 1969 at the age of forty-six, had been particularly reluctant to believe in the reality of the experience lest he appear irrational. "I wish I could think it was an hallucination," he told Dr. Simon when the doctor pressed him. But in the end Barney concluded, "we had seen and been a part of something different than anything I had seen before," and "these things did happen to me." Betty, who continues to speak publicly about her experience, also believes in the reality of these events.[24]

But skeptics remain equally convinced that the Hills' experience was not a real event involving real aliens. Many agree with Dr. Simon that the most likely explanation for this experience lies in the nature of dreams. Others have developed different theories regarding why people might think they have been abducted by aliens, searching for an explanation that does not involve the extraterrestrial.

Chapter 2

After the Hills: Evaluating Abduction Stories

Only one other abduction story was ever published prior to the Hill case. It was a 1965 account concerning Antonio Villas-Boas from Brazil. Villas-Boas claimed that several years earlier he had seen a spaceship land and been given a bizarre physical examination by its alien crew. Ufologists dismissed this account as unbelievable, and it was not publicized.

After the Hill case, abduction stories received more attention. When two men in Pascagoula, Mississippi, reported being abducted and examined in 1973, their story was taken seriously by the media. The same was true for woodcutter Travis Walton in 1975. More abduction cases soon followed. By the 1990s, hundreds of people were calling themselves abductees.

Lies and False Memories

Skeptics, however, believe that the Hill case *caused* all these other abduction reports. In other words, they believe that people who claim to be abductees made up

The cover of this magazine depicts the abduction of two men from Pascagoula, Mississippi, who reported being taken and examined by aliens in 1973.

their stories after reading Fuller's book *The Interrupted Journey* or watching a 1975 TV movie about the Hills. They also suggest that the Hills got the idea for their abduction experience from science fiction movies, television programs, and books. Betty Hill admitted reading a variety of books related to UFOs after her experience, including the book that caused her to write to Donald Keyhoe. She told him: "At this time we are searching for any clue that might be helpful to my husband, in recalling whatever it was he saw that caused him to panic [while driving on the deserted road]. His mind has completely blacked out at this point. Every attempt to recall, leaves him very frightened."[25]

Keyhoe's work concerned the idea of alien kidnappings, and other science fiction stories of the period dealt with aliens experimenting on human beings. Therefore Kevin Randle, Russ Estes, and Wiliam P. Cone say in their book *The Abduction Enigma:* "The elements for the abduction scenario as outlined by the Hills were abundant throughout the media. . . . There is no denying that pop culture had supplied the various elements. Betty Hill may have pulled them together into a single, neat package."[26]

Abduction researchers admit that a few abductees might have been influenced by books or movies about alien abduction, but they insist that most abductees were not prone to read or view such material prior to their abduction experience. Like Betty Hill, they typically seek out such material only after they already suspect that they have been abducted. Moreover, most abductees have no apparent reason to lie or fantasize about abduction.

But many skeptics point out that the majority of abductees—approximately 70 percent, according to some surveys—initially remember their abduction experience during the process of hypnosis. Some ufologists say this means abductees cannot be lying, because hypnosis only uncovers memories of true experiences. But most psychologists agree that hypnotism does not always lead to the truth. In fact, people under hypnosis are just as capable of lying as people not under hypnosis. As Dr. Martin T. Orne, a professor of psychiatry and leading expert on hypnosis, states: "it is possible for even deeply hypnotized subjects to willfully lie [and for] an individual to feign hypnosis and deceive even highly experienced hypnotists."[27]

Skeptics of alien abduction believe that abductees create their own stories based on other publicized abductions.

Abductees can also lie unintentionally while under hypnosis. The human mind is highly unreliable, and people recalling actual events often distort some of the details of what happened. They also sometimes "remember" events that never really occurred. In both instances, they do not realize they are lying.

False memories usually occur because the mind has a need to explain the unexplainable. People search for reasons why things have happened, and when those reasons are not available, they sometimes invent them. For example, a man who discovers a mysterious scar on his arm

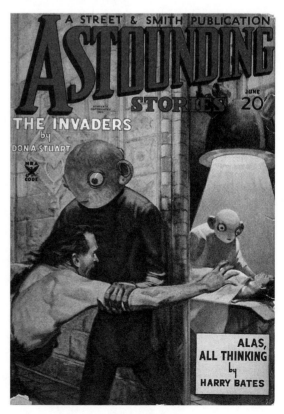

29

might, in trying to explain that scar to himself, wonder whether he fell out of a tree as a child. Over time, he would come to believe that he really did fall out of a tree, and might even remember doing so. Alternatively, he might wonder whether his injury happened on a spaceship during experiments conducted by aliens, and eventually he might subconsciously create a false memory to support his suspicion. To him, this false memory would seem perfectly real.

Psychologists have conducted several experiments to show how false memories become real ones. In one series of studies, people masquerading as robbers burst in on a group and commit a crime. Afterwards the "witnesses" are interviewed about the crime, and their interrogators casually mention false details about what happened. For example, the interrogators might ask how tall the robber with the beard was, when none of the robbers had a beard. Later, when the witnesses are again interviewed about the crime, they typically incorporate the false details into their version of what happened—mentioning, for example, that one of the robbers had a beard. More significantly, the witnesses typically say that they are absolutely certain their memories are correct. They resist any suggestion that they are in error, becoming as insistent as abductees in maintaining their stories' accuracy.

Problems with Hypnosis

Such research suggests that all memories are highly suspect and that the human mind is easily influenced. Moreover, many psychologists believe that false memories are even more likely to be created during the process of hypnosis. An unskilled hypnotist might accidentally prompt a person's response to certain questions, just by the way those questions are asked. In addition, hypnosis can increase people's eagerness to give an appropriate response. Kevin D. Randle, Russ Estes, and William P. Cone explain:

[An] important problem with the use of hypnosis . . . is the desire to please. The prominent abduction researchers claim that the people who come to them have no knowledge of abductions. . . . The truth of the matter is that both the researcher and the client are expecting to learn something that has to do with aliens and abduction. If they have no knowledge, then why seek out an abduction therapist? . . . The power of hypnosis in these circumstances is the subject's desire to please the hypnotist. . . . It is out of this desire that the power of suggestion grows. . . . When the client suggests, after a long session, that nothing else happened . . . the hypnotist keeps pressing until more is found.[28]

Skeptics maintain that abduction researchers are adept not at uncovering abduction memories but at planting them in abductees' minds through hypnosis. But abduction researchers like David Jacobs argue that sessions with abductees show that hypnotism cannot make a person create an abduction experience because "most abductees refuse to be led"[29] during their hypnosis. He offers Betty and Barney Hill as an example, pointing out that although the Hills' therapist Dr. Simon tried many times during their hypnosis sessions to get them to accept their abduction story as merely a dream, they would not. Moreover, Jacobs says that some abductees remember their abduction experience without the aid of hypnosis, and in such cases "their stories are essentially the same as those related while under hypnosis."[30] Jacobs finds this fact important, arguing that if people who are not hypnotized are remembering the same details as those who are, no one can say these details are coming from the subtle hints of a hypnotist.

Common Elements

Many researchers have confirmed that abductees tell similar stories whether or not they are under hypnosis. These stories follow a common sequence of events. Abductee descriptions of the aliens, their ship, and their examination procedures remain fairly constant.

All abductees report being taken from an isolated location, whether it is a deserted road, a forest, or a private home. Jacobs says: "Secrecy appears to be critically important to the aliens in determining the opportunities for abductions. . . . No abductions have surfaced that took place in the middle of a very large group of people, in full view at a public event."[31]

Some abductees went to these secluded places by choice, but others insist they were drawn to them by a sudden, inexplicable urge. One abductee from Ohio says:

> I was driving from Columbus to Marion when I felt compelled to turn into a state park area. I drove into the park about a mile, stopped the car and got out. A bright light was hovering high in the sky over the trees. I stood beside the car and stared at the light. It descended into the trees in front of me. I walked through the trees to the UFO which was sitting on the ground *not* glowing. I went into the UFO.[32]

Most abductees are alone when their experience begins, but a few are part of a small group. In these cases, they report that the aliens chose to abduct only one or two people from the group, leaving the rest behind in some kind of trance. The trance ends when the abductees return.

One example of this concerns the abduction of Will Parker. Parker and his wife Ginny were driving through Virginia late at night when Parker suddenly had the urge to pull into a closed gas station and turn off his engine. The couple heard a noise, and Parker saw an alien approach.

Under hypnosis, he said: "[I see a] little guy, he's outside the car, and he's not human. He's, he ought to be cold because he hasn't got a coat on. . . . Now Ginny is quiet. I'm turning to her, but she's just, she's asleep is what she is. . . . I'm scared for Ginny because I don't know how she's going to, she's not going to remember. . . . [The aliens] told me she's not going to remember."[33] Ginny remained asleep until Parker returned.

Like Parker, most abductees leave quietly with their aliens, whom they say have placed them in another kind of trance. However, some people report a more traumatic experience. Abductee David Masters says of his experience:

A single man climbs out of his vehicle after seeing a UFO descend. Although some abduction stories involve one person, many people recall being with others at the time of abduction.

> Three "people" got out of the small craft. Two of these guys were 4 to 5 feet tall and grey-colored. The other one was brown-colored and much larger than the other two. . . . I began to run. The big brown guy was on me in a flash, forcing me back to the small craft. I resisted and was shocked repeatedly with an "electric" sort of gadget. I continued to resist. They shocked me into unconsciousness. They did so brutally, viciously. I came to and allowed myself to be forced into the small craft.[34]

Aliens in the House

Abductees taken from private homes report similar experiences. They say that aliens entered their rooms on beams of light, usually through windows—open or closed—rather than walls or ceilings. These aliens either examined people within the house or took them to their spaceship first by walking them, carrying them, or floating them away. Greta Lincoln's abduction experience is typical. She reports:

> I was 5 years old . . . [I] awakened for some reason to see seven strange looking forms at the foot of my bed—approximately 4 feet tall, large black eyes round shaped, greyish white skin, large head, very thin body, long arms, fingers and toes. They then seemed to raise me out of the bed without touching me and stayed below up the stairs and outside. There was a very bright light coming down from the sky which seemed to draw us up into it. Next thing I saw was being in a very sterile white room lying on a table with these beings around me again.[35]

Many abductee's stories describe their captors in similar ways. This picture shows the most commonly reported alien form.

Lincoln's description of her captors is similar to those of other abductees. When asked to draw the aliens, many people begin by sketching enormous black eyes in large heads. These eyes are usually almond-shaped with no pupils, irises, or corneas. Most abductees say that aliens have no eyelids and cannot blink. The rest of an alien face appears to be bland. Abductee Judy Kendall says: "[Alien heads] look like ordinary people's heads, but they don't have any hair. No hair anywhere. Their cheekbones are funny-looking. [Their skin is] kind of white and milky. . . . I don't remember seeing a mouth. . . . I don't see any ears . . . all I see is holes."[36]

No abductee remembers seeing alien ears, but some describe a humanlike nose or a slightly raised bump where the nose should be. Many tell of mouths that are either slitlike with no lips or O-shaped with very thin lips. Few abductees see the mouth open, but those who do have noticed a membrane inside. In any case, the mouth doesn't seem to be used for talking. Almost all abductees say that aliens communicate telepathically, mind to mind.

Abductees place aliens in one of two distinct physical categories. One type is small, from two to just over four feet tall. The other is closer to five feet tall. The skin of the smaller aliens has a plastic quality, like a dolphin's skin, while the taller aliens appear rough and leathery. Both groups are physically inferior to human beings. Abductees say that the aliens' strength lies not in their bodies but in their ability to control the human mind and consequently the human body.

While abductees cannot tell one small alien from another, they are able to identify individuals among the taller beings. They say that these aliens have more character in their faces. Abductees believe the tall beings are in charge of the abduction experience. These aliens sometimes wear special clothing, like a white, gray, or black doctor's coat, and direct the work of smaller aliens during physical examinations.

Abductees say the small aliens function as a group to carry out their duties. Together they perform the more menial tasks of an abduction, such as transporting abductees to the spaceship. Both they and the tall aliens work in a businesslike manner and will not be distracted. They ignore human protests but sometimes calm people by staring into their eyes for a prolonged period of time. Abductees say this staring makes them feel very peaceful and seems to eliminate any pain caused by a medical procedure.

Nonetheless, most abductees find their examinations very upsetting. For example, abductee Claire Chambers, a thirty-one-year-old writer, says:

> My boyfriend (age 35) and I were both removed from my bedroom in the night. My large dog attacked and injured one of the aliens. I fought also, but was rendered unconscious. I awoke (in the craft I assume) in a strange environment lying on a table helpless with total paralysis. One alien was by my head and attempted to frighten me with his large eyes. Three other aliens were working on my body. I was terrified and in great pain from the physical procedures they were doing to my body. At one point, I almost strangled and choked to death. I screamed, "NO! STOP! WHY?" over and over. There was no response from the alien life-forms.[37]

The Physical Examination

Examinations take place in small, circular rooms with strange machines, metallic-looking floors, and white and gray walls. Sometimes abductees begin their experience sitting in a narrow, curved waiting room with benches in the walls.

Aliens usually begin their examinations at the feet and work their way up. Absolutely no area is left untouched. Aliens scrape human skin, snip off pieces of hair, and look inside eyes, ears, nose, and throat. Sometimes they use machinery similar to X-ray equipment. According to abductee Tom Murillo:

> I was raised up into the spacecraft . . . where I landed on a glass-like table. I lay [there] for a few moments till these four tall aliens came into the room. They observed me for a while, then started

their examination on me. A scanning device was used all the time. This device went around the glass table—above, sideways, under the table—and all the time I couldn't move a muscle except my eyes. All the data picked up by the scanning device was fed into a strange-shaped grey screen where I was fortunate to see my insides. My heart, my stomach, and other parts. I just lay there as I was examined.[38]

Many abductees report that the aliens end the examination with the placement of a small, round object deep inside their nose or ear. Sometimes they remove an object instead. David Jacobs says that this implant has some kind of important purpose. It "might be a locator so that the targeted individual can be found and abducted; it might serve as a monitor of hormonal changes; it might facilitate the molecular changes needed for transport and entrance; it might facilitate communication."[39] Many ufologists believe it is a tagging device similar to the one Earth scientists use to track animals for long-term study.

Commonly, abductees describe aliens implanting a small object in their noses or ears. Various hypotheses have been developed regarding the purpose of this object.

Some abductees claim to have been abducted more than once. Repeat abductees often report that the same tall alien has been present at every one of their abductions. They say these aliens notice anything that has changed since the last abduction. For example, one abductee tells Jacobs that the aliens showed concern when she dyed her hair from black to blonde. Another says that the aliens were puzzled after she got braces on her teeth and removed a sample of tissue from her gum.

Abductees say aliens usually take tissue samples from the leg, arm, or back. Their incision can be long and thin, wide and messy, or scoop-shaped. In addition, several male abductees report having their sperm collected. Female abductees often say the aliens have used a long needle to extract ova or implanted them with embryos that are removed during a later abduction.

Hybrid Children

Many abductees also insist they have seen half-human, half-alien children among the aliens. Some of these hybrids are fetuses in incubators that look like fish tanks with blue liquid in them. Others are young children in a nursery with four or five "nanny" aliens looking after them.

Most abductees who have seen these hybrids report that they are listless and sickly. Several abductees say that the aliens have told them they have to hold these children because they need a human's touch. Abductee Jill Pinzarro says: "It's very important, and [the aliens] can't do it. [The child] needs it from me. [The aliens] can't give it what it needs completely. It's sort of a species-specific need, I guess."[40] Other abductees say that the hybrids need not just touch but also human interaction. These abductees report that the aliens encouraged them to play with the children, talk to them, or hold them.

Abductee descriptions of these children vary greatly. Some babies seem more human, some more alien, but in every instance the infant is clearly a mixture of both.

Abductee Debbie Jordan describes the child she believes was made using one of her ova:

> The little girl was about the height of a four-year-old child, but she was very tiny otherwise. She had tiny ears, set low on her head, a tiny mouth, and large blue eyes. Her forehead was very large and her body seemed very thin and frail. She had snow white hair that was patchy on her large head and her complexion was very pale. . . . [When she blinked, her] eyeballs rolled back and her eyelids met in the middle of her eyes.[41]

Psychological Tests

Some abductees have not seen any of these hybrid children. Their abduction experiences center around alien psychological tests. They say that the aliens made them watch scenes on a screen or visualize scenes in their minds. These scenes evoked an emotional response, either disturbing or pleasant. Abductee Karen Morgan says that the aliens made her visualize her mother's death and that during this visualization, an alien was "telling me that I [had] to feel the way I did then. . . . It [was] very emotional, and he [was] making me watch it . . . like it [was] just all happening again."[42] During such a procedure, a tall alien typically stares into the abductee's eyes, apparently to study his or her reactions.

The aliens conduct other tests as well. Some of these tests determine manual dexterity. Others evaluate memory. A few examine the human pain threshold. In addition, some abductees claim that the aliens have transferred knowledge into their brains. However, these abductees cannot recall the knowledge. They say it has been hidden for future use.

Once all the tests are done, the abduction experience ends abruptly. Most abductees say that the aliens rushed them from the spacecraft to return them to the site of their abduction. Sometimes this process happens so quickly that the abductee ends up in a slightly wrong place.

At this point, most abductees forget their experience. Budd Hopkins believes this forgetfulness serves to protect an alien research study. He says:

> Memory blocks may . . . have to do with the abductee's role as a "human specimen" unwittingly being studied over a period of years. If people are being picked up as children, implanted with monitoring devices, and abducted a second time after puberty, at the very least the first abduction would have to be concealed. If the study is truly long range, the subjects would have to be kept in the dark about their role for many years, and a strongly effective block would have to be imposed.[43]

Like Budd Hopkins, many people believe the abduction experience is real because abductee descriptions are similar, consistent, and full of detail. However, skeptics still challenge them, saying only physical proof is irrefutable. Many ufologists are therefore trying to find hard evidence that aliens exist.

Chapter 3

The Search for Physical Proof

Ufologists want to find definite proof of alien abduction. To this aim, they have studied abductees' minds as well as their bodies. They have also examined UFO sightings, hoping to find evidence that alien spacecraft are indeed visiting Earth.

One of the first steps in looking for proof of an abduction is the polygraph or lie detector examination, which researchers use to find out whether a particular abductee is telling the truth. A polygraph examination uses a machine to detect certain changes in the human body that occur when a person is lying. When abductee Whitley Strieber took such a test, the results indicated he was not lying about having had an abduction experience. However, as Strieber himself admits, a polygraph examination does not prove an abduction has really taken place. It merely shows that the abductee *believes* it has taken place. Strieber states: "My successful completion of this test in no way proves that my recollection of my experiences

Author and abductee Whitley Strieber took a polygraph examination that showed he was not lying about his abduction story. Such a test is often a first step in proving truth of an abductee's story.

is correct, but it does confirm that I have described what I saw to the best of my ability."[44]

In addition to the polygraph examination, researchers sometimes administer psychological tests to determine an abductee's mental stability. The results of such tests have led some psychologists to conclude that most abductees are surprisingly normal. For example, Dr. Aphrodite Clamar, who interviewed the abductees mentioned in Budd Hopkins's book *Missing Time*, says she discovered nothing unusual about any of Hopkins's subjects:

> I did not find any drug users among the subjects whom Budd Hopkins brought, nor any alcoholism, nor any strange habits . . . . Persons who claim to have had UFO experiences . . . come in all sizes, shapes, ages, and sexes. . . . [They] are run-of-the-mill people, neither psycho nor psychic, people like you and me. I could find no common thread that ties them together—other than their UFO experience—and no common pathology; indeed, no discernible pathology at all.[45]

Nonetheless, skeptics still insist that abductees are mentally unbalanced. They remind us that these people often have emotional problems, which psychologists label Post-Abduction Syndrome. Skeptics think PAS does not come from being abducted but is instead a sign of a hidden psychological disorder that actually causes the sufferer to *think* that he or she has been abducted.

Physical Signs

However, abductees who claim to have experienced alien surgical procedures do exhibit scars on their bodies. Many ufologists say this proves without a doubt that alien abductions are real. Physicians cannot explain these scars, which sometimes seem surgically precise and can appear inside the nose or within internal organs. Moreover, some of these scars are quite unusual. For example, one thirty-six-year-old abductee interviewed by researcher Kenneth Ring exhibited marks the day after experiencing an alien medical procedure. This woman explains:

> Under closer examination I noticed that they were three small blisters in the shape of a triangle. It really frightened my husband and me. I couldn't concentrate on anything all day. Later that night when taking my bath I noticed that the blisters had dried up somewhat and turned black. (Now they are still visible like burn scars.)[46]

Some skeptics believe that such scars were caused by long-forgotten, ordinary childhood events, while others suggest that the human mind could be creating them. Researchers know that people can control their blood pressure and other bodily functions through mental techniques like biofeedback and meditation. Followers of the Christian religion sometimes exhibit spontaneously occurring wounds, called *stigmata*, on

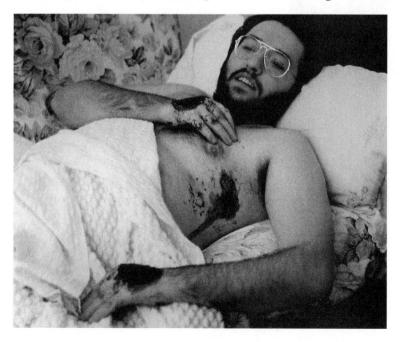

Italian stigmatic Giorgio Bongiavanni lies in bed with bleeding wounds. Many researchers use examples of stigmatics to support their belief that people can affect skin tissue through thought.

their hands and feet. These Christians believe their wounds were made by God to remind them of Jesus Christ's crucifixion. Nonbelievers say stigmata are proof that human thought can affect skin tissue.

Alien Implants

Skin tissue changes might account for another physical sign of abduction: alien implants. Some abductees have felt objects beneath their skin or seen them in X rays of their bodies and consequently insisted that the objects were put there by aliens. In the case of abductee Richard Price, one of these objects worked its way loose from his skin in June 1989. He gave it to David Pritchard, a scientist at the Massachusetts Institute of Technology (MIT), who analyzed the object and reluctantly decided it was not alien in nature. According to Pritchard, the object was made of "the kind of material elements and chemicals—carbon, oxygen, hydrogen, and compounds—one would expect if the object were biological in origin and formed right here on planet Earth."[47]

Thomas Flotte of Massachusetts General Hospital in Boston agrees. Flotte, a pathologist with a specialty in skin, says the human body itself is capable of producing such an object whenever an item like a piece of glass or a wood splinter is lodged beneath the skin. The body attacks the foreign substance by wrapping it in layers of fibroblasts, which are a type of cell found in connective tissue. This covering becomes hardened, or calcified, and according to Flotte "this calcification process is com-

It is nearly impossible to prove whether or not an implant like the one shown here is truly of alien character.

mon."[48] In Price's case, within the calcified covering was a cotton fiber that had become incorporated into the tissue as it hardened. Pritchard speculates that this fiber came from Price's underwear.

Still, MIT scientist Pritchard acknowledges that aliens *could* have made the object, constructing it in such a way that it looked like calcified tissue in order to deceive people. He says: "It's possible that the aliens are so clever that they can make devices that serve their purposes yet appear to have a prosaic origin as natural products of the human body and fibers from cotton underwear. So this case only rules out the possibility of clumsy aliens. It doesn't rule out the possibility of super-clever aliens."[49]

Other cases of suspected alien implants have also turned up unusual cocoons of tissue around these objects, but it is unclear whether the human body could have made them. In discussing tissue samples from several implant-related surgeries, Dr. Roger Leir reports that they contained nerve cells that would not be expected in such an area. Moreover, the tissue did not show the inflammation that Leir would expect to see given that the body was reacting to a foreign body. Dr. Leir writes:

> I found no medical literature that entertains the possibility that a foreign substance can be lodged in a human body without the surrounding flesh reacting to it. Our system of defense . . . comes into play the moment a foreign object enters our body. This system of defense is designed to ward off any invading substance, thus providing the body with the protection it needs.[50]

Therefore Leir speculates that aliens could have created the unusual cocoons as a way to protect their implant devices from being rejected by the human body.

Leir examined several of these suspected implants during a series of surgeries in 1995 and 1996. He removed these objects from several patients, documenting the operations with photographs, videotape, and live witnesses. One of his criteria for selecting patients for his study was that they had presented their abduction stories without the aid of hypnosis. Leir explains his reasoning for this:

> Critics and debunkers of the alien abduction phenomenon point disapprovingly to the retrieval methods of investigators. Their first criticism focuses on the use of regressive hypnosis. . . . Although there are many well-qualified individuals performing hypnosis, there has never been a professional standard developed for the best method of memory retrieval. In a world full of complexities such as false memory syndromes . . . we must adopt research criteria that are beyond reproach.[51]

An abductee known only as Annie is typical of Dr. Leir's patients. He introduces her case:

> Annie . . . appeared to be a classical textbook case of alien abduction, with all the signs that are known to appear. In addition, she had a signed affidavit from her neighbor across the street attesting to the fact that on the same night an alleged abduction experience occurred to Annie, she had witnessed a circular-shaped craft hovering over Annie's house. This sincere surgical candidate was able to clearly recall numerous details that occurred during her abduction experiences. She also had a demonstrable lesion on the skin of her leg, which was red in color and raised. She described the history of the lesion and how her doctor had treated it. She had had a small surgery performed to drain the area, which resulted in delayed healing that took the better part of a year. She said that the doctor drained a copious amount of a purple fluid . . . and was mystified

about its origin. . . . X-rays of the area demonstrated an object that appeared essentially as a small radio-opaque ball located in the soft tissues just below the area of involvement on the skin. We decided to remove the skin lesion and all the tissue below, including the foreign object shown on the X-ray.[52]

The object that Leir removed from Annie was, he reports, "a small, round, greyish-white ball."[53] Later analysis showed that it was comprised of a number of metals, including an iron core, but could not determine what it was. Another suspected implant was far more unusual. Removed from a patient named Patricia, it was T-shaped and contained at least eleven different elements—sodium, aluminum, barium, silicon, lead, calcium, copper, iron, nickel, manganese, and silver—along with some mineral traces. Leir had the object analyzed by an independent laboratory without telling its technicians the origin of the object. The laboratory subsequently reported that the object most likely came from a meteor and had many characteristics consistent with an "extraterrestrial origin."[54]

California podiatrist Roger K. Leir actively tries to locate and study alien implants.

However, the report also states that the object could be an iron sliver that accidentally became embedded in the patient's skin and was somehow transformed by the body—although the report does not speculate on how this might have occurred. Leir believes that this second possibility was added after laboratory workers told him the object was extraterrestrial and he excitedly revealed it came from one of his patients. He believes that the laboratory personnel were not comfortable supporting the idea that alien implants are real.

The Roswell Connection

During the course of his research, Dr. Leir was given a piece of metal by an anonymous source who said it came from the crash of an alien spaceship near Roswell, New Mexico, in 1947. The Roswell incident has received a great deal of publicity over the years. At the time it occurred, the U.S. military said that the object that crashed during a thunderstorm was a weather balloon. Other people, however, believe that the U.S. government concocted the weather balloon story to cover up the truth: that the military recovered alien debris and bodies at the crash site.

People who visited the crash site before the military arrived to remove the "balloon" debris later insisted they saw four alien bodies there. Other witnesses claim to have seen these aliens after they were taken to a nearby military base. A local mortician insists he got a phone call from someone there asking how to preserve the aliens' bodies. Both a nurse and a pathologist claim to have examined the dead aliens, and several military officers contend they saw the pathologist's report, which included photographs of the aliens. One woman, Norma Gardner, says that she typed the autopsy reports and saw the alien bodies once they had been preserved in a chemical solution. All of the witnesses provide the same basic description of the aliens, one which is strikingly similar to descriptions provided by abductees. The aliens were hairless, slightly less than five feet tall, and had large heads with big eyes, slits instead of ears, and a tiny mouth with no lips. Their bodies were skinny, their arms long, their legs short.

In all, more than 350 people have talked about seeing the aliens or their spaceships at Roswell, and others—some of them military officers—have reported hearing details about the alien craft and its occupants. Yet the government continues to deny that the debris at Roswell came from anything other than a weather balloon. Nonetheless, when

Major Jesse Marcel, an intelligence officer at Roswell Army AirField, holds the remains of a so-called flying disk.

Dr. Leir had the piece of debris analyzed in 1997, he learned that it contained some elements commonly found in meteors. The scientist who supervised the analyses, Dr. Russell VernonClark, discovered that the sample includes silicon in a far greater concentration than would naturally occur on Earth. Moreover, the object displays a uniform structure that suggests it is not a meteor but was instead designed by some intelligent being. Dr. VernonClark therefore says that it is likely "this material is both manufactured and extraterrestrial in origin."[55] Abduction researcher Darrel Sims, who also worked on the investigation, adds:

> Whether or not the subject of extraterrestrial intelligence is in your belief systems, the scientific evidence

49

. . . , combined with the history of the debris, has led us to the conclusion that something of extraterrestrial origin, whether a vehicle or not, was in fact present in the desert outside Roswell in July of 1947.[56]

Skeptics, however, point out that there is no hard evidence that the sample actually came from Roswell. They suspect a hoax, although they have not yet offered suggestions as to how the strange object could have been created by those perpetrating the hoax.

Damaged Soil

Similar accusations have been made against those claiming they have evidence of a spaceship landing. These claims relate to circular areas of damaged ground, which some abductees argue is proof that a spaceship landed on the ground near the site of their abduction. For example, abductee Kathy Mitchell says that after a UFO appeared in her backyard, she saw "an eight-foot circle of dead grass . . . with a swath of dead grass coming from the circle in a perfectly straight path that was approximately two feet wide and forty-eight feet long."[57] Mitchell says that the circle remained "unchanged after months of fertilizing, watering, and reseeding"[58] and lasted for five years, during which time all animals avoided it. She adds that "the ground inside the circle and strip repelled not only water, but any new life, including weeds. . . . The dirt in the affected area was like ground-up cement."[59]

Ufologist Budd Hopkins investigated this circle. He photographed it and took two soil samples from Mitchell's yard, one from inside the circle and one from outside it, and then sent both samples to a laboratory for analysis. The laboratory then tried to make the normal soil match the damaged soil by subjecting it to extreme heat. In his book *Intruders*, Hopkins reports that "it was necessary to heat the unaffected sample in an oven at 800 degrees

Fahrenheit for six hours to achieve the same color as that of the affected soil, though without duplicating its solidified appearance. Clearly, the amount of energy emitted by *something* [at the location of the circle] was enormous, though we have no idea of its nature."[60]

However, skeptic Philip Klass says this circle might have been caused by nothing more than a simple fungus. He states:

> Some centuries earlier, the visible aftermath of this fungus, which dehydrates the soil so nothing will grow there and which often takes on an irregular circular shape, was given the name "Fairy Ring" because some superstitious folk assumed that it was a playground for tiny fairies. Today, for many UFOlogists, such Fairy Rings have become the mark of UFO landing-sites.[61]

A similar circle that appeared in Medford, Minnesota, in November 1975 was not caused by fungus. At that time, the Kay family reported that a UFO had landed at a nearby football field. Investigators later examined the area and took soil samples from the landing site. These samples were analyzed at the University of Kansas Space Technology Laboratory, which determined that the landing-site soil emitted ten times more heat and light than the normal soil, although it looked the same as the normal soil when viewed under a microscope.

Photographic Evidence

Another type of hard evidence related to alien abductions are photographs of UFOs that have been taken in areas where abductions have been reported. However, in every instance, skeptics have insisted these photographs can be explained by photographic errors or are outright hoaxes. In fact, UFO photographs are relatively easy to fake, and many frauds have been perpetrated by people eager to create their own proof of UFOs. Fake UFO photographs have also been produced by debunkers—people who will go to great lengths to discredit those who believe in UFOs. If a debunker can get a ufologist to say that a fake UFO photo is real, that debunker can then expose the fake and destroy the ufologist's credibility. According to Ed and Frances Walters, who have written extensively about abductions in Gulf Breeze, Florida, "motivated UFO debunkers go to a lot of trouble in their efforts to ridicule the UFO phenomenon. Discrediting real UFO photographs with their fake photographs is a common practice used by debunkers to influence negative stories in the media."[62]

Ufologists therefore examine any UFO photographs they receive from the public very carefully. They use computers to analyze UFO images for hidden strings, unusual shadows, or other evidence of fakery. Over the years, the equipment for such electronic analysis has become more sophisticated. Many ufologists now feel confident about declaring some UFO photographs authentic.

Although UFO photos do exist, many, like this one, have proved to be fake.

However, given the thousands of UFOs sighted in the sky each year, skeptics say that if UFOs are real there should be more than just a few authentic photographs of them. Ed Walters disagrees, arguing that most people don't carry a camera with them at times when they would see a UFO. He explains: "We could equate the odds of seeing a UFO to the possibility of seeing an automobile accident or some other newsmaking event and realizing that you don't have a camera with you. . . . [Actually] I am impressed with the number of quality photographs that have been taken."[63]

Gulf Breeze, Florida

In addition to photographs, UFOs have also been captured on videotape, particularly in Gulf Breeze, Florida. An ABC news crew filmed a UFO in the skies over Gulf Breeze on January 11, 1991. Another was filmed there on May 10, 1991, by a Japanese crew from the NIPON television network. In fact, there have been so many sightings over Gulf Breeze that ufologists call the entire Gulf Strip area a "UFO hot spot." Witnesses involved in these UFO sightings include police officers, local government officials, and a retired Air Force F-4 pilot.

Gulf Breeze is also the reported site of an abduction experience. Ed Walters says that after an episode of missing time he underwent hypnosis and recalled being abducted from the community several times. According to Walters, the aliens placed a strange apparatus on his head that made him recall certain events in his life. He explains: "The visions were rapid and took me on an emotional roller coaster ride. . . . For reasons unknown to me, I was being forced to relive experiences in my life which involved intense emotion."[64] Walters writes that the aliens triggered "four different feelings perhaps unique to humans, Joy, Love, Grief, and Pride."[65]

Walters has no doubt that his abduction experience really happened, and he is frustrated when people say they don't believe him. After all, he argues, he has taken many photographs of UFOs flying over Gulf Breeze. Isn't this definite proof that aliens have visited his community?

Skeptics say it is not. They have called Ed Walters a liar and accused him of using a model of a spaceship to fake UFO photographs. In fact, in 1990 a reporter covering a Mutual UFO Network International Symposium on the Gulf Breeze phenomenon found such a model at Ed Walters's former home. Walters insists that the model is the wrong size and shape to produce the UFOs seen in the photographs and suggests that debunkers manufactured the model themselves in order to discredit him. But skeptic Jacques Vallee attacks Ed Walters's reputation and calls the entire Gulf Breeze phenomenon "sleazy."[66] The publicity resulting from the area's UFOs has led Vallee to believe that Walters and other residents manufactured their photographs just so they and their community would become famous.

Even ufologists admit that a desire for fame and attention have caused some people to falsify hard evidence of alien abduction. However, they argue that the body of evidence is too large to be explained only by hoaxes. Meanwhile, some psychologists and ufologists have focused their abduction research on the human mind, rejecting the search for hard evidence in favor of studies into the psychology of alien abduction. These researchers believe that the key to understanding the abduction phenomenon lies in the nature of abductees rather than aliens.

Chapter 4

Abductions and the Human Mind

People unwilling to believe that aliens from another planet are visiting Earth typically say that unless fraud is involved, alien abductions occur only within the human mind. They say abductees are causing their experience themselves, through imagination or other mental processes.

The harshest skeptics suggest that abductees need serious psychological help. Others attribute abduction experiences to fantasy rather than mental illness. For example, psychologists Sheryl C. Wilson and T. X. Barber say "that there exists a small group of individuals (possibly four percent of the population) who fantasize a large part of the time, who typically 'see,' 'hear,' 'smell,' and 'touch' and fully experience what they fantasize; and who can be labeled fantasy-prone individuals."[67] But abduction researchers disagree with the idea that all abductees are fantasy-prone. For example, David Jacobs says: "The abduction phenomenon has no strong element of personal fantasy. . . . Most abductees' lives contain nothing that would have such a strong effect upon them that they would hallucinate a full-scale, copiously detailed abduction event that they desperately do not want to have."[68]

Brain Activity

Like Jacobs, psychiatrist Kenneth Ring rejects the idea that abductees have fantasy-prone personalities. Instead he argues that they have encounter-prone personalities. In other words, abductees are not more likely to fantasize than anyone else. They are just more likely to encounter something strange. Ring explains that in this respect abductees have many traits in common with people who share mystical or visionary experiences. Such people accept the possibility that the world is not always as it seems and are interested in alternative explanations for reality. They know that unusual things can happen in life.

Neuroscientist Michael Persinger has noted that encounter-prone people tend to have frequent electrical surges in areas of the brain known as the temporal lobes. In comparison to people who do not have such surges, these people report a much higher incidence of paranormal or mystical experiences. According to skeptics Theodore Schick Jr. and Lewis Vaughn: "Persinger has actually induced such experiences—including abduction-like experiences—in people by applying magnetic fields across the brain, thereby instigating bursts of electrical activity."[69] Schick and Vaughn also report:

> Earthquakes, which produce strong magnetic effects, could trigger temporal lobe surges. So Persinger predicted that reports of UFO abductions and sightings would correspond to the dates of seismic activity. When he tested his prediction, he found that he was right; there was a strong correlation between seismic events and the weird experiences.[70]

Schick and Vaughn believe that Persinger's research is strong evidence that the mind is causing the perception of alien abductions. Others, however, point out that not every abduction experience takes place after an earthquake and that not all abductees experience brain surges. Moreover, there are other things that encounter-prone personalities have in common that could be used to explain their experiences.

Childhood Trauma

For example, many encounter-prone individuals have suffered childhood trauma or abuse. Ring theorizes that this abuse caused them to develop "an extended range of human perception beyond normally recognized limits."[71] In other words, a person who is suffering great pain must use all of his or her mental power to endure it. Perhaps this mental effort heightens the senses. Could it be that abuse victims are able to see and hear things that others can't see or hear?

Other researchers think this idea of heightened senses is nonsense. However, they do agree that someone who was abused as a child is more likely to report being abducted by

Neuroscientist Michael Persinger has done research demonstrating that the brain activity of people likely to experience paranormal events differs from those who have never experienced such happenings.

57

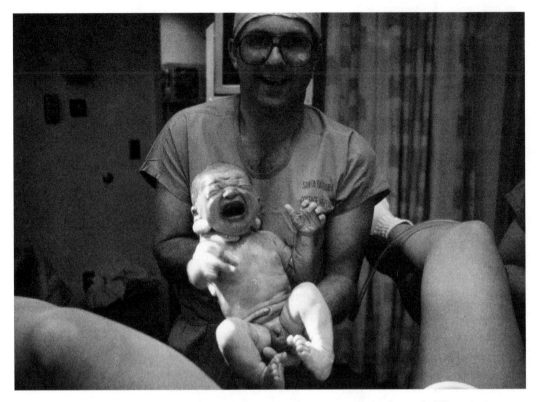

Some researchers believe that alleged abductees are in fact remembering their own births.

aliens than someone who was never abused. They interpret this to mean that child abuse somehow creates abduction memories in adulthood. Many studies suggest that childhood suffering is not always remembered the way it really happened; the mind recalls the trauma in a distorted way. In abduction stories, this might mean that the aliens represent human beings who hurt the abductees years ago. Jacobs explains: "[This] theory postulates that the victims are so traumatized by abuse they suffered as children that they forced the incidents out of their conscious memory; now, years later, the painful memories have resurfaced in disguised form."[72]

Perhaps as adults, people who consider themselves to be abductees have simply transformed their memories of childhood abuse into abduction scenarios. Just as they were once helpless children in the hands of capricious, violent adults, now they are helpless adults in the hands of cold, uncaring aliens. This child-abuse theory is accepted by many psychologists and skeptics. However, Jacobs believes it to be false. He argues that many abduction memories relate to adult rather than childhood events. He also accurately points out that not all abductees have been abused and some have no history of any kind of childhood trauma.

But some researchers argue that all people have suffered a childhood trauma. Simply by being born, everyone has experienced pain. These researchers think that alleged abductees are people remembering their own births. Since this memory is deep and difficult to access, most people can't recall it at all. However, some psychologists believe that people are capable of remembering it symbolically. Under this theory, abductees have simply transformed their memory of birth into a memory of abduction.

This birth-trauma theory suggests that the dark tunnel of the alien spaceship might really be the dark tunnel of the birth canal. At the end of the tunnel, the aliens' brightly lit examining room might be the hospital room where babies are delivered, and the strange, mouthless aliens might symbolize human doctors wearing medical masks. However, all births are different, and babies delivered by the surgical procedure of cesarean section do not travel down a dark passage. Infants born with their eyes closed do not see the doctors or the delivery room. Because of these variations in birth experiences, David Jacobs says:

> The minds of newborn abductees would have to contain countless bits of specific identical information relating to their birth environment, regardless of whether their eyes were closed, whether they were born in a dark area, whether other people were present, and so forth. Presumably, all babies would retain the endless details of many other "traumatic" events as well.[73]

Jacobs also argues that if people were able to remember their own births, even symbolically, then they would also be able to remember other painful infant events, such as vaccinations. Some people who support the birth-trauma theory think that this is indeed the case. They suggest that the mind combines memories of early medical procedures with the ones related to birth. In other words, memories of medical examinations and procedures from infancy transform doctors into aliens in the human mind. Abduction stories therefore result from an infant's view of all medical examinations.

However, a few proponents of the birth-trauma theory do not think the aliens symbolize human doctors. These researchers say that when alleged abductees are describing aliens they are really remembering other newborns they saw in the nursery right after being born. They argue that aliens look too much like human fetuses to be anything else.

Similarly, some people suggest that the supposed abductees might be remembering their own image as fetuses. Perhaps there is some kind of mirror effect in the womb. But ufologist Raymond Fowler says this is ridiculous, adding: "Most embryologists would totally discount the theory that a fetus would have the ability to see his own image."[74] Fowler argues that the birth-trauma theory does not adequately explain why abductees say aliens look the way they do. Abductee descriptions are very specific, rich in detail, and surprisingly consistent. Many abduction researchers, including Fowler and Jacobs, consider this proof that the aliens are not some kind of symbolic memory but real creatures.

The Imaginal Realm

But psychiatrist Kenneth Ring argues that the word *real* needs redefining. He thinks that aliens do exist, but in another reality from our own. Ring has decided that the abduction experience is one of several mystical and visionary states within the human mind. People who are in one of these states are connected to another reality.

Ring calls this reality the imaginal realm. The imaginal realm is another world, "the cumulative product of imaginative thought itself,"[75] and exists as an actual place. In his book *The Omega Project*, Ring quotes a French Islamic scholar, Henry Corbin, who says:

> [I]t must be understood that the [imaginal] world . . . is perfectly real. Its reality is more irrefutable and more coherent than that of the empirical world where reality is perceived by the senses. Upon returning, the beholders of this world are perfectly aware of having been "elsewhere". . . . For this reason we definitely cannot qualify it as being imaginary in the current sense of the word, i.e., unreal or nonexistent. [The imaginal] world . . . is ontologically as real as the world of the senses and that of the intellect. . . . We must be careful not to confuse it with the imagination identified by so-called modern man with "fantasy."[76]

Psychologist Kenneth Ring believes that alien abductees have experienced a visit to another world he calls the imaginal realm.

Ring explains that people in the imaginal realm have "imaginal bodies" and seem as solid as we are. Up until now, however, most of us have been unable to see them. Ring thinks abductees are people who have suddenly found themselves able to see creatures from the imaginal realm. They have learned how to bridge the gap between two realities.

Ring believes that the human mind is evolving to allow this to happen. Because of evolution, he claims, more and more people will someday be able to contact creatures from the imaginal realm. In fact, he sees the abduction phenomenon as the first sign that humans are undergoing a shift in consciousness that will allow people to move back and forth at will between two worlds, the physical and the imaginal.

The Near-Death Experience

Ring developed his theories about the abduction experience and the imaginal realm while investigating near-death experiences. A near-death experience is reported when doctors are able to revive someone who has been clinically dead. Upon awakening, these near-death experiencers (NDErs) sometimes tell stories that Ring finds strikingly similar to abduction memories.

Just as abductees talk about walking or floating down a spaceship tunnel to a brightly lit examining room, NDErs say they floated out of their bodies and traveled down a long tunnel with a bright light at the end of it. Therefore Ring believes that during the near-death experience, NDErs have entered the same imaginal realm as abductees. He says some of them have also seen the abductees' "aliens." As one NDEr told him: "There was a light toward the end of the tunnel but before I could reach it, two figures appeared outlined in light. They communicated with me through my mind, telepathically. I recognized one of the figures as being my father. He confirmed and agreed with everything conveyed by his companion who seemed to have great authority, like an angel or one of God's helpers."[77] Ring compares the telepathic powers of these angels to those of abductees' aliens.

Ring believes that even though abductees and NDErs reach the imaginal realm through different means, they share the same altered mental state while there. Abductees begin to see creatures from the imaginal realm on their own, while NDErs can only do so after the death process has forced them into a new reality. Another thing that abductees and NDErs have in common is that they both leave the imaginal realm with a feeling that the Earth's environment is in trouble. Abductees often report that the aliens showed them pictures of Earth being destroyed by an environmental disaster. Similarly, during death many NDErs see a vision of global disaster. As a result, abductees and NDErs both come away from their experience with a greater concern for Earth.

Abductees and NDErs also both leave the imaginal realm with a heightened sense of spirituality. Ring's studies reveal that both groups "report becoming more altruistic, having greater social concern, and increasing in spirituality."[78] They show an "appreciation for life, self-acceptance, concern for others, [a decrease in] materialism, [and a] quest for meaning and spirituality."[79] However, Ring adds that this does not mean these people will become more involved with a particular religion after their experience. In fact, a majority of them abandon organized religions to follow a more universal doctrine of beliefs, typically criticizing organized religions for dividing rather than uniting all human beings.

Ring expected to find that NDErs came away from their experience with heightened spirituality. After all, they had been brought back to life from the dead. But he was surprised to find that people abducted by aliens would say this made them more spiritual too. He eventually traced abductees' spirituality to a belief that the aliens were sent to Earth to help rather than harm its people. Most of the abductees Ring interviewed said: "There are higher order intelligences that have a concern with the welfare of our planet."[80] Some of these people felt the aliens were sent to Earth by God.

A painting depicts an abduction experience. Some abductees believe that aliens watch out for life on Earth and that they are sent by God.

Ring believes that spirituality is a key component of the imaginal realm. He points out that modern people have lost touch with mythology and magic. Perhaps the abduction experience is a way for people to return to their spiritual roots. He points out that many tribal cultures have ancient rituals requiring an individual to leave the group and undergo some kind of trial. Stories about abduction and near-death experiences sound somewhat similar to these rituals, in that they involve a person traveling to an otherworldly place and returning with a new outlook on life.

Ring believes that the abduction phenomenon fulfills the same purpose. It encourages human beings to evolve to a higher level of consciousness. Abductees see creatures that no one else sees. Therefore Ring thinks abductees are experiencing the next stage of human evolution. But many abduction researchers reject the idea that the human mind can create aliens in an imaginal realm. For example, David Jacobs does not believe that the human mind can create real aliens who inhabit another realm—and even if this were possible, he argues, why would anyone want to create aliens?

If . . . [this were] possible, then human beings would be creating many alternative realities and would have been doing so for all time. But the creation of an alternative reality that would terrorize its creator, cause her to experience physical damage, and then make her live in fear that it will happen again seems unreasonable when people might instead create physical realities wherein their deepest pleasurable fantasies could be played out. No evidence whatsoever has been presented to suggest that this theory has any viability.[81]

The Collective Unconscious

Because of the level of terror connected to abduction experiences, some people have compared alien abductions to nightmares. In fact, some psychologists believe that aliens are created not in an imaginal realm but in dreams, noting that many alleged abductees first recover their memories of aliens while asleep. As for why all dreamers would create the same vision of an alien, psychologists have discovered that everyone's dreams contain the same basic images, regardless of a person's culture; these common images, called archetypes, symbolize people's deepest desires and fears. Some believe that these archetypes are based on memories inherited from previous generations.

In other words, human genes pass on more than just hair color or eye color; they contain ancient memories stored within a part of the mind that proponents of this theory call the collective unconscious. If the collective unconscious exists, abductees might not be seeing real aliens but archetypal images, and abduction stories might be symbolic dreams that reflect deep-seated emotions and other mental experiences passed down from earlier generations.

Aliens as Folklore

The concept of a strange being from another world has existed since ancient times in every culture, but it originally

Folklore often describes non-humans like fairies or gods capturing humans. These stories are similar to abduction stories.

appeared in folklore. Sometimes these alien creatures were called fairies; other times they were called gods. Whatever their names, these strange beings typically had the capacity to overpower or trick unsuspecting human beings. In many stories, they show themselves to certain human beings and not others, and in some stories they take people to an otherworldly place. For this reason, Peter Brookesmith, an expert in UFO sightings, concludes:

> My own conviction is that the human mind is inextricably involved with all UFO phenomena, from "simple" sightings of flying disks to complex, full-blown abduction accounts. I say this partly because of the astonishing variety in UFO reports, and partly because UFOs and aliens seem to single out individuals or small groups of people to whom they reveal themselves—while remaining unseen by others close by. But mainly I say it because the secret history of the UFO stretches back into antiquity.

The similarities between modern UFO reports and ancient tales of fiery wheels, dragons and portents in the sky are truly remarkable; moreover, there are extraordinary parallels between today's descriptions of abductions by aliens and archaic accounts of folk being "stolen" by elves and goblins.[82]

But there is an alternative explanation for why these parallels exist. Perhaps ancient stories about elves and goblins were true—and perhaps these beings were really aliens from another planet. Cave drawings indicate that the idea of aliens has existed since prehistoric times—and where else but from reality would a Stone Age human get the idea for an alien? As French ethnologist Aimé Michel says:

> For, as long as modern UFOs are nothing more than fantasy, invented by fools who have read too much science fiction . . . we must accept that early man filled his head with too much bad literature, or how else would he have gotten the idea of preserving for eternity [in his cave art] flying saucers with an unheard of precision? If man had invented them, and . . . [the government] tries to prove that the similar appearances . . . were only weather balloons, . . . hallucinations and such, then we can equally well believe that UFOs from the time of the [Stone Age] culture were airplanes and weather balloons.[83]

This historic rock carving in Italy is said to depict an astronaut. Such rock carvings are used as evidence that aliens and UFOs have always existed.

Michel has studied the artwork in seventeen prehistoric caves in France and seen images that look strikingly like UFOs and aliens. Others have discovered ancient writings that mention alien abductions. For example, the Abbé de

Villars, a French monk who lived from 1635 to 1673, wrote in his book *Comte de Gabalis* about an incident reported in the ninth century that sounds much like an abduction story. He says that several air vehicles appeared in the sky, and then:

> When it became clear to the air beings to what extent they had excited the people and what animosity they had evoked, they lost their senses to such an extent that they landed their big ships and took some of the best men and women on board to teach them and dispel the bad opinion the people had about them. . . . But, when these men and women came back to the earth, they were regarded as demonic beings who had come to spread poison on the fields. So, they were quickly arrested and, after being put through the worst forms of torture prescribed for those who practice the arts of the devil, they were executed. . . . Besides that, at Lyons [in France], three men and a woman were seen to come out of one of these air vehicles. The whole town gathered around them and called out, "They're magicians! . . . [An enemy] has sent them to destroy . . . [us]. The four innocent ones explained that they too belonged to the same country and had been kidnapped by strange beings, who had shown them unbelievably wonderful things and requested them to spread the news of that.[84]

Stories like this, which existed long before space travel or science fiction novels, have convinced many people that aliens are not fantasies or imaginary beings but real creatures who have visited Earth for centuries. But if aliens are real, and if they do come from another planet, why would they be visiting Earth? What could they hope to achieve by contacting us? Why do they behave in such mysterious ways? These questions have produced a variety of theories from those who have carefully studied abductees' stories.

Chapter 5

Why Would Aliens Be Visiting Earth?

People who accept the idea that real aliens are visiting Earth have developed several theories regarding the purpose of the alien visits, most of them based on the details of alien behavior found in abduction stories. Of course, experts in alien abduction acknowledge that their theories are mere speculation based on their own biases. As ufologist Raymond Fowler points out:

> My dog might see me out in my garden, digging. From his point of view, he probably thinks I'm looking for a bone. Each one of us is looking at one facet or two facets of the UFO phenomenon and saying, "I like that! It seems to fit." Things that don't fit, we ignore. The "alien agenda" is built on what seems acceptable to the researcher, and everything else is rejected.[85]

Research Studies

Perhaps the most prevalent theory regarding why aliens are visiting Earth is that they are akin to human zoologists who

A typical scene of aliens studying a human. Many abductees and researchers alike believe that aliens abduct humans to study and learn about them.

study wild animals. Says abductee Kathy Mitchell: "If you compare a UFO abduction to the capture and testing of wild animals to record their migration and living habits—sedation, capture, examination, and tagging for future identification—you will find striking similarities."[86] Abductee Mac McMahon also compares aliens to zoologists, saying that their approach to their research "wasn't an antihuman attitude, it was more of a We're going to check you out, pup. Get up there on the table sort of deal. I get the same impression when I take a dog to the vet."[87]

This suggests that the aliens might be conducting a research study on human beings. Perhaps the abductees' implants are monitoring devices related to this study. As ufologist Budd Hopkins says:

> One inescapable inference to be drawn from this
> pattern is that a very long-term, in-depth study is

being made of a relatively large sample of humans, and that this study may involve mechanical implants of some sort. . . . If such a long-term monitoring system is going on, it would help explain the decades of surreptitious UFO behavior and the absence of direct communication.[88]

In fact, the aliens' behavior would be consistent with this type of purpose, given what we know about how humans go about such studies. As Dr. Edgar Mitchell, an astronaut who walked on the moon during the second landing there, says of his own experience on a strange world:

> If we had expected to encounter any kind of living beings, which, of course, we didn't, we would naturally have asked NASA to put us down in some very unpopulated region where we could examine the local fauna in safety and at our discretion. We would have wanted to pick up some living specimens, examine them, and put them back with a minimum of fuss, hoping to get back to Earth safely with as much information as possible.[89]

Similarly, some people suggest that the aliens are studying human society and are perhaps engaging in certain behaviors in order to lessen the chance that those who report seeing them will be believed. Ufologist Johannes von Buttlar explains:

> An open contact would disturb our society and its dynamics and influence it to such an extent that the results of the aliens' observations of it would be contaminated. Our anthropologists also try to keep to a minimum their influence on a society they wish to observe. Extraterrestrial intelligences would perhaps, therefore, prefer to restrict their

contacts to individual encounters so as to camouflage their reconnaissance as far as possible. Perhaps they have even deliberately staged the meaningless scenarios reported by the so-called contactees [people who say they have received messages from aliens], so that their reports do not find general acceptance and they are mostly regarded as fools or psychopaths.[90]

Genetic Material

The prevailing view among many experts at the forefront of abduction research, however, is that the aliens' main goal is to extract genetic material from abductees. However, the aliens' motivation for this behavior is in dispute. Some people, like ufologist Michael Mannion, believe that the aliens might be collecting genetic material in order to understand why human beings behave the way they do, perhaps as part of a study of humans' destructive tendencies. He says:

> The great question—*what ails mankind?*—remains unanswered. If intelligent alien beings were studying humanity, is it not likely that they too would seek to find the answer to that question, an answer that has eluded mankind for thousands of years? If so, where might they look? It is quite possible that in studying the human animal, an alien culture might begin at the beginning—gestation, the period of development in the uterus from conception until birth. Perhaps, they might reason . . . that the answer to what plagues the human animal may begin in the uterine environment. Or the problems may stem from events surrounding birth or which occur in the immediate period after birth.[91]

But ufologist Budd Hopkins suggests that the aliens might instead be conducting some type of genetic experiments. He says:

> Can an advanced technology, whose home base is outside Earth, be experimenting . . . with various human genetic combinations? Our own present-day science has successfully mated sperm and ovum in a test tube, implanted the fertilized egg in a female body, and brought the fetus to term. Cloning is a much talked about area of current experimentation, moving slowly from lower animal forms towards man himself. There is no way to estimate what a radically advanced technology might be capable of.[92]

Hopkins further suggests that the aliens might be coming to Earth to steal something that we don't yet find significant ourselves but which is of great value to them. He explains:

> What if the UFO occupants are *taking* something from their captives? Many people assume . . . that if alien beings could travel across distances ranging upwards from four light-years (the distance of the nearest star, Alpha Centauri, from Earth) then they must indeed be supermen, and the idea is therefore ludicrous that they might need anything we possess. Even more outrageous, they add, is the idea that extraterrestrials might be afraid of us, or vulnerable in any way. But why assume any of these things? We may indeed possess something—a natural resource, an element, a genetic structure—that an alien culture might desire to use, for example, as experimental raw material.[93]

Many abductees and ufologists believe that the aliens have somehow become unable to produce their own genetic material and need ours. David Jacobs says: "One of the purposes for which UFOs travel to Earth is to abduct humans to help aliens produce other Beings. It is not a program of reproduction, but one of *production*. They are not here to help us. They have their own agenda, and we are not allowed to know its full parameters."[94]

Other experts in alien abduction do not see why the aliens would need to keep abducting people to improve their gene pool. Given a little genetic material and foreseeable technological advances, even human beings might one day be able to duplicate, or clone, human beings without having to kidnap so many people. Moreover, most abductees are average people—neither top athletes nor gifted with higher-than-average intelligence. A few even have health problems that can be passed on genetically and would be undesirable in a gene pool.

But some people believe that the aliens are not concerned with physical characteristics but emotional ones. For example, an abductee named Peter reports that the aliens "want our love and how it is we love and care and have such compassion. They also are terrified of our anger and our ability to hate and kill and all that stuff, and they're trying to get the two apart."[95] Peter says that through genetics the aliens hope to take "the higher human qualities and separate them from the lower human qualities and somehow . . . reincorporate them into our race . . ."[96] The hybrid children created by the aliens would therefore be superior to humans emotionally if not physically.

Earth's New Inhabitants

Many abductees believe that these hybrid children are meant to inhabit Earth after human beings have become extinct due to some kind of global disaster. Some abductees claim that the aliens have communicated this information to them through thoughts, either during the abduction experience or later when they were back at home. John Mack tells of an abductee named Scott who says a disaster will someday destroy all human life. Mack says Scott believes: "Major changes in the world are coming. . . . The aliens will only come 'when it's safer.' But that will not occur until there are 'less and less' of us as we die off from disease, especially more communicable forms of AIDS that will reach plague proportions."[97]

Other abductees have suggested that the aliens might be trying to create their idea of the perfect Earth inhabitant. Such a creature would possess human strength and size along with only the most positive human emotions; it would never be violent. By creating strong yet passive humans, the aliens might be trying to make willing slaves. Alternatively, they might be trying to save Earth from the damage that normal humans do to the environment and to each other.

The latter is the prevalent view among abductees. Typical is the opinion of an abductee named Carlos who says the aliens are specimen collectors who just want to protect Earth's environment. Carlos describes the aliens as being "like little tiny drones of a vaster complexity" who are "in the service of survival."[98] He thinks that some higher power or divine being has told the aliens to keep Earth from "collapsing."[99] That's why the aliens warn abductees not to destroy their environment, and perhaps why they are genetically changing human beings. Carlos says the aliens are "Earth gardeners trying really hard to instruct us to find a plenitude and not to be caught in the human impulses towards extinction."[100] He believes the aliens want people to discover that "plenitude in the environment, a plenitude of the garden Earth."[101]

Another abductee, Betty Andreasson Luca, also believes that the aliens want to save Earth. She says that they "are the *caretakers* of nature and natural forms—*The Watchers*. They love mankind. They love the planet Earth

Abductee Betty Andreasson Luca poses with representations of extraterrestrial creatures she claims to have encountered. Luca believes that aliens have good intentions and are trying to save the Earth.

and they have been caring for it and man since man's beginning. . . . Man is destroying much of nature."[102] Luca also suggests that aliens abduct the same subjects repeatedly in order to monitor the effects of environmental damage on the human body and to find ways to repair this damage. People who share this view argue that it explains why the number of alien abductions increased during the 1970s and '80s, when environmental pollution was severe but humans were not yet doing much to address the problem.

A Symbolic Dream

But Kenneth Ring, who remains convinced that aliens exist only in the imaginal realm, suggests that the aliens' environmental warnings are symbolic messages sent from one human mind to another. In his view, alien examinations of human beings represent our own evaluation of what we are doing wrong as a species. Philosopher Michael Grosso agrees with this position, saying:

I cannot help thinking it is we who are in need of dire examination; it is we who have to place ourselves on an "operating table." It looks to me as if something—some intelligence—is "examining" and "operating on" us. Medical operation implies a need for healing. The latest development in UFO symbolism [that is, the abduction narrative] contains a message about healing ourselves.[103]

Ring asks: "What is it in ourselves that needs healing?"[104] He finds his answer in the image of the alien itself, "frail and tortured-looking, his enormous black eyes reminding us, as Grosso observes, of the images we have all seen on our television screens . . . of children dying of starvation in drought-plagued Africa."[105] The aliens represent human suffering.

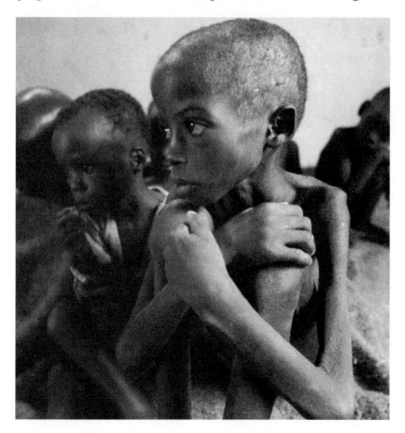

The appearance of these malnourished Rwandan orphans is similar to the typical description of an alien. Therefore some researchers believe that aliens represent human suffering and are a message to heal world problems like starvation.

George C. Andrews is another believer in the theory that aliens are trying to convey messages to help life on Earth.

Ring is suggesting that our imaginations have created the aliens to show us what might happen if we don't change our ways. These aliens have come from the imaginal realm to warn us that if pollution continues, our future children will look like them. Ring says:

> The future of the human race—symbolized by the archetype of the child—is menaced as never before. We need to heal ourselves of all those tendencies—unthinking greed, mindless development, ruthless exploitation—that threaten our native habitat so severely as to make us fear that our progeny will be replicas of the stunted and deformed aliens that now infiltrate the collective nightmare that portions of humanity are dreaming.[106]

Grosso suggests that the hybrid babies in abduction stories further equate aliens with human babies. He explains:

Taken literally, the reason [for the hybrid babies] perhaps is to revitalize *their* ailing stock. Taken symbolically, the idea of hybrids would be about *our* need to be revitalized; the need to enhance our gene pool. It certainly makes sense to say that we need to embark on evolutionary experiments, to mutate *ourselves*. In other words, if we interpret the symbolism of the abduction experience as a strange kind of species dream, the message is that our world, symbolized by the otherworld, is a dying wasteland and that we have to evolve into a higher (and hence more adaptable) species.[107]

Psychic Telegrams

Researchers like Ring and Grosso think that human minds are the source of the aliens' environmental warnings. So does George C. Andrews. However, Andrews does not think our minds have *created* the aliens. Instead he thinks our minds have *called* them.

In his book *Extra-Terrestrials Among Us*, Andrews suggests that human beings have been mentally broadcasting their concerns about the environment throughout the universe. He speaks of "psychic telegrams" sent to "telepathic" aliens out in space—"a telepathic S.O.S. Mayday call for help to save the planet's biosphere."[108] He speculates that some ancient power within the Earth itself might even be sending "distress signals through space."[109] Has Earth called the aliens here to stop human destruction? Andrews says:

Are those distress signals what the UFOs have come in response to? Has Mother Earth asked to have her face cleaned? Have we been transforming our planet into a cancer cell in the body of the galaxy instead of making it the garden of the universe? Perhaps the Christian, Islamic, Hebrew, Mazdean and Hopi traditions of Judgment Day refer to the day when the Earth is once more "relieved of its heavy load."[110]

Religious Connection

Many other experts in alien abduction have found a religious aspect to the abduction phenomenon. Ufologist Brad Steiger says:

> In my opinion, the UFO contactees, with their emphasis upon spiritual teachings being transmitted to Earth by Space Beings, are seeking to bring "God" physically to this planet. These UFO prophets have created a blend of science and religion that offers a space-age theology that seems more applicable to a good many modern men and women.[111]

Steiger is suggesting that the aliens represent both modern science and ancient religion. He is convinced that this combination is important to today's society. In recent times, many people have rejected religion because they feel it conflicts with science. They embrace technology but stop believing in God. As a result, they feel that human beings are alone in the universe.

Steiger points out that the existence of aliens would change that feeling. If abductees are right, then human beings must consider themselves part of a greater purpose. God might not have a plan for them, but the aliens do. Steiger says we need this outlook on life:

> In our day of fear and dread, in our time of endless chaos, pollution, fallout, rips in the ozone layer and threats of nuclear annihilation, we need a sense of meaning and purpose for existence as never before in our history as a species. If, as contact with extraterrestrial intelligences would seem to suggest,

we are not alone in the universe, then life does have a meaning, for we now have the opportunity to become part of a larger community of intelligences. We may now become evolving members in a hierarchy of cosmic citizenship.[112]

To Steiger, it doesn't matter whether the aliens are real or not. It doesn't matter where they come from. Regardless of their origin or identity, their words and purpose are the same. He says: "Whoever or whatever the Space Beings may be—whether cosmic missionaries or projections of the Higher Self—the channeled [that is, telepathically transmitted] messages which they share may be the scriptures and theological treatises of the New Age."[113]

Steiger is proposing that the aliens' messages are the doctrine of a new religion. This doctrine tells human beings how to live—just as the doctrines of traditional religions do. For this reason, Dr. Gordon Melton, director of the Institute of the Study of American Religion, compares abductees to religious disciples, saying that UFO contactees represent "an emerging religious movement with an impetus and a life of their own."[114]

But the aliens' religious doctrine does not just concern environmental issues. Both abductees and people who say they have received alien messages from afar claim these creatures want to change our entire way of life. Steiger reports:

Contactees have been told that the Space Beings hope to guide Earth to a period of great unification, when all races will shun discriminatory separations and all of humankind will recognize its responsibility to every other life form existing on the planet. The Space Beings also seek to bring about a single, solidified government, which will conduct itself on

A computer-generated image of a threatening alien. Many people claim that aliens should not be viewed as invaders, but as guardian angels.

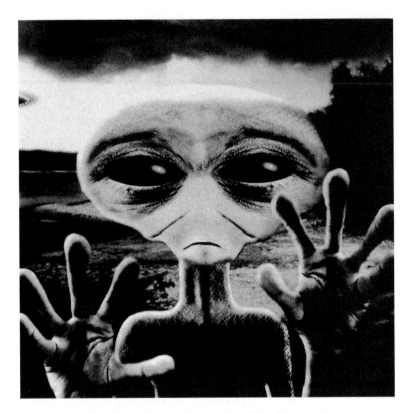

spiritual principles and permit all of its citizens to grow constructively in love.[115]

According to Steiger, it is this emphasis on love and racial harmony that has led some people to equate the aliens with guardian angels. Such comparisons convince him that religion has to be an important part of UFO study. Ufologists cannot ignore the religious significance of the abduction experience. Steiger says:

However one deals with the Flying Saucer Movement in one's own reality, the undeniable fact remains that thousands of men and women throughout the world have made the UFO a symbol of religious awakening and spiritual transformation. Some envision the UFO as their deliverer from a world fouled by its own inhabitants.[116]

Steiger concludes that the explanation for the aliens is not as important as the experience of the aliens. We should not be spending our time arguing about the aliens themselves. Instead we should be listening to what abductees are saying about their messages.

John Mack shares a similar view. He accepts that we may never know where aliens come from or what they really are. But he believes that even if aliens remain a mystery, abduction stories can still teach us a great deal. They tell of an environmental tragedy that might be avoided. They warn people to change their way of life. They offer different visions of the future. Certainly these messages deserve consideration. Mack says:

> The alien beings have come to the abductees from a source that remains unknown to us. We still do not fully grasp their purposes or their methods. . . . Some have speculated that the alien beings have mastered time travel and come to us from the future. Sometimes they even communicate that this might be so. We do not know. But the guiding or regenerative myth of the abduction phenomenon offers a new story for a world that has survived many holocausts and may yet be deterred from a final cataclysm [world-ending event]. The abduction phenomenon, it seems clear, is about what is *yet to come*. It presents, quite literally, visions of alternative futures, but it leaves the choice to us.[117]

Notes

Introduction: Are Alien Abductions Real Events?

1. Kevin D. Randle, Russ Estes, and William P. Cone, *The Abduction Enigma*. New York: Tom Doherty Associates, 1999, pp. 70–71.
2. Raymond E. Fowler, *The Watchers: The Secret Design Behind UFO Abduction*. New York: Bantam, 1990, pp. 352–53.
3. Philip Klass, *UFO Abductions: A Dangerous Game*. Buffalo, NY: Prometheus Books, 1989, p. 6.
4. Michael Mannion, *Project Mindshift: The Reeducation of the American Public Concerning Extraterrestrial Life 1947–Present*. New York: M. Evans, 1998, p. 296.
5. Mannion, *Project Mindshift*, p. 296.

Chapter 1: Suspecting Abduction: The Hill Case

6. Quoted in John G. Fuller, *The Interrupted Journey: Two Lost Hours "Aboard a Flying Saucer."* New York: Dial Press, 1966, p. 30.
7. Quoted in Fuller, *The Interrupted Journey*, p. 30.
8. Klass, *UFO Abductions*, p. 9.
9. Fuller, *The Interrupted Journey*, pp. 31–32.
10. David M. Jacobs, *Secret Life: Firsthand Documented Accounts of UFO Abductions*. New York: Simon & Schuster, 1992, p. 248.
11. Debbie Jordan and Kathy Mitchell, *Abducted!* New York: Carroll & Graf, 1994, p. 15.
12. Jacobs, *Secret Life*, p. 217.
13. Jacobs, *Secret Life*, p. 217.
14. Fowler, *The Watchers*, p. 266.
15. Quoted in Fuller, *The Interrupted Journey*, pp. 158–59.
16. Quoted in Fuller, *The Interrupted Journey*, pp. 162–63.
17. Quoted in Fuller, *The Interrupted Journey*, p. 164.
18. Quoted in Fuller, *The Interrupted Journey*, p. 176.
19. Quoted in Fuller, *The Interrupted Journey*, p. 187.
20. Quoted in Fuller, *The Interrupted Journey*, pp. 187–88.
21. Klass, *UFO Abductions*, p. 11.
22. Klass, *UFO Abductions*, p. 12.
23. Budd Hopkins, *Missing Time*. New York: Ballantine Books, 1981, p. 16.
24. John E. Mack, *Abduction: Human Encounters with Aliens*. New York: Ballantine Books, 1994, p. 447.

Chapter 2: After the Hills: Evaluating Abduction Stories

25. Quoted in Randle, Estes, and Cone, *Abduction Enigma*, p. 126.
26. Randle, Estes, and Cone, *Abduction Enigma*, p. 126.

27. Quoted in Klass, *UFO Abductions,* pp. 57–58.
28. Randle, Estes, and Cone, *Abduction Enigma,* p. 337.
29. Jacobs, *Secret Life,* p. 291.
30. Jacobs, *Secret Life,* p. 291.
31. Jacobs, *Secret Life,* p. 50.
32. Quoted in Jacobs, *Secret Life,* p. 80.
33. Quoted in Jacobs, *Secret Life,* pp. 64–65.
34. Quoted in Kenneth Ring, *The Omega Project: Near-Death Experiences, UFO Encounters, and Mind at Large.* New York: William Morrow, 1992, pp. 72–73.
35. Quoted in Jacobs, *Secret Life,* p. 71.
36. Quoted in Hopkins, *Missing Time,* p. 64.
37. Quoted in Ring, *The Omega Project,* p. 79.
38. Quoted in Ring, *The Omega Project,* p. 82.
39. Jacobs, *Secret Life,* p. 95.
40. Quoted in Jacobs, *Secret Life,* p. 171.
41. Quoted in Jordan and Mitchell, *Abducted!,* p. 243.
42. Quoted in Jacobs, *Secret Life,* p. 144.
43. Hopkins, *Missing Time,* p. 223.

Chapter 3: The Search for Physical Proof

44. Whitley Strieber, *Communion: A True Story.* New York: Avon Books, 1987, p. 304.
45. Quoted in Hopkins, *Missing Time,* p. 236.
46. Quoted in Ring, *The Omega Project,* p. 76.
47. Quoted in Patrick Huyghe, "Alien Implant or—Human Underwear?" *Omni,* April 1995, p. 47.
48. Quoted in Huyghe, "Alien Implant or—Human Underwear?" p. 47.
49. Quoted in Huyghe, "Alien Implant or—Human Underwear?" p. 48.
50. Roger Leir, *The Aliens and the Scalpel.* Columbus, NC: Granite Publishing, 1998, pp. 152–53.
51. Leir, *The Aliens and the Scalpel,* p. 45.
52. Leir, *The Aliens and the Scalpel,* p. 109.
53. Leir, *The Aliens and the Scalpel,* p. 118.
54. Leir, *The Aliens and the Scalpel,* p. 229.
55. Quoted in CNI News, "The Artifact: Is This Extraterrestrial Material?" www.cninews.com/CNI_Artifact.html, p. 10.
56. Quoted in CNI News, "The Artifact," p. 4.
57. Jordan and Mitchell, *Abducted!,* p. 20.
58. Jordan and Mitchell, *Abducted!,* p. 20.
59. Jordan and Mitchell, *Abducted!,* p. 20.
60. Quoted in Budd Hopkins, *Intruders: The Incredible Visitations at Copley Woods.* New York: Ballantine Books, 1987, pp. 49–50.
61. Klass, *UFO Abductions,* p. 91.
62. Ed Walters and Frances Walters, *UFO Abductions in Gulf Breeze.* New York: Avon Books, 1994, p. 284.
63. Walters and Walters, *UFO Abductions in Gulf Breeze,* p. 291.
64. Walters and Walters, *UFO Abductions in Gulf Breeze,* p. 93.
65. Walters and Walters, *UFO Abductions in Gulf Breeze,* p. 95.
66. Jacques Vallee, *Revelations: Alien Contact and Human Deception.* New York: Ballantine Books, 1991, p. 187.

Chapter 4: Abductions and the Human Mind

67. Quoted in Klass, *UFO Abductions,* p. 201.
68. Jacobs, *Secret Life,* p. 290.

69. Theodore Schick Jr. and Lewis Vaughn, *How to Think About Weird Things*. Mountain View, CA: Mayfield Publishing, 1999, p. 257.
70. Schick and Vaughn, *How to Think About Weird Things*, p. 257.
71. Ring, *The Omega Project*, p. 146.
72. Jacobs, *Secret Life*, p. 285.
73. Jacobs, *Secret Life*, p. 301.
74. Fowler, *The Watchers*, p. xxii.
75. Ring, *The Omega Project*, p. 219.
76. Quoted in Ring, *The Omega Project*, p. 220.
77. Quoted in Ring, *The Omega Project*, p. 101.
78. Ring, *The Omega Project*, p. 175.
79. Ring, *The Omega Project*, pp. 175–76.
80. Ring, *The Omega Project*, p. 189.
81. Jacobs, *Secret Life*, p. 301.
82. Peter Brookesmith, *UFO: The Complete Sightings*. New York: Barnes & Noble Books, 1995, p. 8.
83. Quoted in Michael Hesemann, *UFOs: The Secret History*. New York: Marlowe, 1998, p. 227.
84. Quoted in Hesemann, *UFOs*, p. 243–44.

Chapter 5: Why Would Aliens Be Visiting Earth?

85. Quoted in Mannion, *Project Mindshift*, p. 288.
86. Jordan and Mitchell, *Abducted!*, p. 185.
87. Quoted in Hopkins, *Missing Time*, p. 112.
88. Hopkins, *Missing Time*, p. 210.
89. Quoted in Hopkins, *Missing Time*, p. 16.
90. Quoted in Hesemann, *UFOs*, p. xiv.
91. Mannion, *Project Mindshift*, p. 293.
92. Hopkins, *Missing Time*, p. 215.
93. Hopkins, *Missing Time*, p. 211–12.
94. Jacobs, *Secret Life*, p. 304.
95. Quoted in Mack, *Abduction*, p. 306.
96. Quoted in Mack, *Abduction*, p. 306.
97. Quoted in Mack, *Abduction*, p. 92.
98. Quoted in Mack, *Abduction*, p. 363.
99. Quoted in Mack, *Abduction*, p. 363.
100. Quoted in Mack, *Abduction*, p. 363.
101. Quoted in Mack, *Abduction*, p. 363.
102. Quoted in Fowler, *The Watchers*, p. 202.
103. Quoted in Ring, *The Omega Project*, p. 226.
104. Ring, *The Omega Project*, p. 226.
105. Ring, *The Omega Project*, p. 226.
106. Ring, *The Omega Project*, p. 226.
107. Quoted in Ring, *The Omega Project*, p. 227.
108. George C. Andrews, *Extra-Terrestrials Among Us*. St. Paul, MN: Llewellyn Publications, 1986, p. 291.
109. Andrews, *Extra-Terrestrials Among Us*, p. 291.
110. Andrews, *Extra-Terrestrials Among Us*, p. 291.
111. Brad Steiger, "UFO Contactees— Heralds of the New Age," *Unsolved UFO Sightings*, Winter 1995, p. 57.
112. Steiger, "UFO Contactees," p. 57.
113. Steiger, "UFO Contactees," p. 57.
114. Quoted in Steiger, "UFO Contactees," p. 57.
115. Steiger, "UFO Contactees," p. 60.
116. Steiger, "UFO Contactees," p. 59.
117. Mack, *Abduction*, p. 421.

For Further Reading

Gary L. Blackwood, *Alien Astronauts*. New York: Benchmark Books, 1999. Part of a series called "Secrets of the Unexplained," this book presents information on UFO and alien sightings.

Peter Hepplewhite and Neil Tonge, *Alien Encounters*. New York: Sterling Publications, 1998. This book discusses UFO sightings, beginning with the famous Roswell, New Mexico, case.

Judith Herbst, *The Mystery of UFOs*. New York: Atheneum, 1997. This book offers a history of UFO sightings, beginning in ancient times, and gives possible explanations for what people saw.

Brian Innes, *Alien Visitors and Abductions*. Austin, TX: Raintree Steck-Vaughn, 1999. This book offers a skeptic's views on UFO sightings and alien abductions.

Larry Kettelkamp, *ETs and UFOs: Are They Real?* New York: William Morrow, 1996. This book discusses over a dozen famous cases of UFO sightings and alien abductions.

Works Consulted

George C. Andrews, *Extra-Terrestrials Among Us*. St. Paul, MN: Llewellyn Publications, 1986. Andrews believes that aliens are real and offers his own unique views on why they might be visiting Earth.

Peter Brookesmith, *UFO: The Complete Sightings*. New York: Barnes & Noble, 1995. Brookesmith presents information on many UFO-related events throughout history.

CNI News, "The Artifact: Is This Extraterrestrial Material?" www.cninews.com/CNI_Artifact.html. This website offers information regarding an analysis of materials present in pieces of debris suspected to have come from a crashed flying saucer.

Raymond E. Fowler, *The Watchers: The Secret Design Behind UFO Abduction*. New York: Bantam, 1990. Fowler discusses several cases of alien abduction and suggests that the aliens might be attempting to help human beings.

John G. Fuller, *The Interrupted Journey: Two Lost Hours "Aboard a Flying Saucer."* New York: Dial Press, 1966. Fuller reports on his experiences interviewing abductees Betty and Barney Hill.

Michael Hesemann, *UFOs: The Secret History*. New York: Marlowe, 1998. Ufologist Michael Hesemann offers a thorough discussion of UFO-related issues in modern times.

Budd Hopkins, *Intruders: The Incredible Visitations at Copley Woods*. New York: Ballantine Books, 1987. Well-known abductee and ufologist Budd Hopkins describes a series of alien abductions in Indianapolis.

Budd Hopkins, *Missing Time*. New York: Ballantine Books, 1981. Hopkins reports on several cases of alien abduction and offers his own views regarding the cause of such experiences.

Patrick Huyghe, "Alien Implant or— Human Underwear?" *Omni*, April 1995. Huyghe discusses a unique case involving a suspected alien implant.

David M. Jacobs, *Secret Life: Firsthand Documented Accounts of UFO Abductions*. New York: Simon & Schuster, 1992. Jacobs reports on his interviews with abductees and offers his own theories regarding what might be causing the alien abduction phenomenon.

Debbie Jordan and Kathy Mitchell, *Abducted!* New York: Carroll & Graf, 1994. Jordan and Mitchell describe their own experiences as abductees.

Philip Klass, *UFO Abductions*. Buffalo, NY: Prometheus Books, 1989. Skeptic Philip Klass argues that there are no real aliens.

Roger Leir. *The Aliens and the Scalpel*. Columbus, NC: Granite Publishing, 1998. Leir describes his experiences as a surgeon removing strange objects from abductees' bodies and provides photographs of these objects.

Elizabeth Loftus, and Katherine Ketcham, *The Myth of Repressed Memory*. New York: St. Martin's Press, 1994. This work discusses False Memory Syndrome in depth.

John E. Mack, *Abduction: Human Encounters with Aliens*. New York: Ballantine Books, 1994. This book presents Mack's interviews with abductees and his theories regarding the reasons for the alien abduction phenomenon.

Michael Mannion, *Project Mindshift: The Reeducation of the American Public Concerning Extraterrestrial Life 1947–Present*. New York: M. Evans, 1998. This book suggests that the U.S. government knows that aliens are visiting Earth and have been using the popular media, including television programs like *Star Trek*, to prepare people to accept the aliens when they reveal themselves.

Kevin D. Randle, Russ Estes, and William P. Cone, *The Abduction Enigma*. New York: Tom Doherty Associates, 1999. This book examines a wide variety of current research into the abduction phenomenon and suggests that its origin lies within the realm of human psychology and culture.

Kenneth Ring, *The Omega Project: Near-Death Experiences, UFO Encounters, and Mind at Large*. New York: William Morrow, 1992. Ring presents his research into alien abductions and suggests that abductees are people capable of accessing an alternate reality.

Theodore Schick Jr. and Lewis Vaughn, *How to Think About Weird Things*. Mountain View, CA: Mayfield Publishing, 1999. Schick and Vaughn cast a critical eye on a variety of unusual beliefs, including the belief that aliens are abducting human beings.

Brad Steiger, "UFO Contactees—Heralds of the New Age," *Unsolved UFO Sightings*, Winter 1995. Steiger discusses alien abductions in terms of religious beliefs.

Whitley Strieber, *Communion: A True Story*. New York: Avon Books, 1987. Strieber describes his own experiences as an abductee.

Jacques Vallee, *Revelations: Alien Contact and Human Deception*. New York: Ballantine Books, 1991. Vallee suggests that much of what we know about aliens has come from carefully planned hoaxes.

Ed Walters and Frances Walters, *UFO Abductions in Gulf Breeze*. New York: Avon Books, 1994. The authors describe Ed's abduction experiences and talk about other abductions near their home in Gulf Breeze, Florida.

Index

Picture Credits

About the Author

Patricia D. Netzley received a bachelor's degree in English from the University of California at Los Angeles (UCLA). After graduation she worked as an editor at the UCLA Medical Center, where she produced hundreds of medical articles, speeches, and pamphlets.

Netzley became a freelance writer in 1986. She is the author of over two dozen books for children and adults, including *The Curse of King Tut* and *UFOs* for Lucent Books. She and her husband, Raymond, live in southern California with their children, Matthew, Sarah, and Jacob.